To Mum

The Promises of Giants

How YOU can fill the leadership void

John Amaechi OBE

NICHOLAS BREALEY
PUBLISHING

London • Boston

First published by Nicholas Brealey Publishing in 2021
An imprint of John Murray Press
A division of Hodder & Stoughton Ltd,
An Hachette UK company

1

A CIP catalogue record for this title is available from the British Library

Hardback ISBN 9781529345872
eBook ISBN 9781529345902 UK / 9781529345926 US

Typeset by KnowledgeWorks Global Ltd.

Printed and bound in Great Britain by Clays Ltd, Elcograf S.p.A.

John Murray   renewable
and recyclabl   ustainable
forests. The   pected to
conform to t   of origin.

John M   lishing
Carme   oup
50   er 53,
Emb:
London   USA

Contents

Foreword

In many ways I am ill-suited and ill-equipped to write this foreword. Although I have had the pleasure of working with John over the years, John would not count me as one of his close friends or work colleagues. I am not an organizational psychologist, and I'm no use at team sports. I am a white, late-fifties, slightly stocky, straight male with a full head of hair.

So we are fabulously different!

However, that may be precisely why John has asked me to write this foreword. As someone responsible for the strategy of a very large, purpose-led professional services business, I have had the privilege of observing John's work and influence, both within our own organization and with global corporates.

His work and this book are nothing short of arresting.

Take the time to read and reflect on this book, and in addition to discovering some wonderful things about John and his mum, you should also start to reflect more on yourself, your choices, your impact and influence, and the impact and influence you have on your friends, family and your own organizations.

Resist any temptation to skim *The Promises of Giants* and chalk it up as another book devoured. Instead, listen to the book, and listen to yourself as you read it. It will cause you to appraise and even confront your good self. You will start to weave a giant's coat.

Slowly, gems and nuggets will wash up which you will sew into your giant's coat. Gems like what winning is all about, that boldness and vulnerability are twins, or that vigilance is an essential weapon against bias. Nuggets for your business life, helping you to think again about the people you might not always pay attention to, seeking out those in your organization at the vanguard of change, or finding antidotes for dealing with insurgents!

By the end, your giant's coat will be an intricate weave of your own choices and promises as well as your organization's culture. If your promises are *The Promises of Giants*, you will wear your coat lightly, with conviction, humility and integrity.

Alastair Morrison
Pinsent Masons
London

Introduction

Some of you reading this might have a vague awareness of who I am from my ten-year career playing professional basketball. Or from my first book, *Man in the Middle*, and the rush of publicity that accompanied my "coming out." Being the first openly gay former NBA player is still what I'm best known for, and probably always will be. An unfortunate truth, given that the bit about being gay required zero effort on my part.

Since my retirement from sport in 1995, I've worked a lot harder for what I believe are far greater accomplishments. So, to reintroduce myself, my name is John Amaechi, and I am the founder of APS, a professional consultancy that is now in its twentieth year of operation. We have a brilliant staff and a diverse client list that includes industry titans from across all sectors. We are welcomed into the inner sanctums of senior management teams and the rank-and-file, and together we work to identify and apply evidence-based and practical solutions to the most vexing challenges that face organizations today.

In addition to my work with APS, I am a member of the Occupational Psychology Division of the British Psychological Society; a Chartered Scientist and Science Council Member with the Institute of Science Technology; a research fellow at the University of East London Department of Psychology; a director of the Manchester University NHS Foundation Trust and our nine area hospitals and community services; a contributing writer with the British Psychological Society; and an Officer of the Most Excellent Order of the British Empire (OBE), awarded for contributions to charity and sport.

I appreciate that you *don't* need this level of detail. For most of you, those titles and affiliations are mere words on a page. But I've become accustomed to leading with my credentials because I know they are not what people see when they first look at me. What they initially see is what people have always seen, ever since I was a child: an awe-inspiring and/or terrifying giant.

I could be presented to an audience with the most grandiose of introductions and a recitation of my accolades that is even more extensive than the list above, but the first reaction, no matter the size of the group or the context of the gathering, will always be absolute bewilderment.

Wow. He is tall. He is really, really tall. I don't believe I've ever seen someone so tall. How tall must he be, exactly?

You will have to do an Internet search for that, I'm afraid. That's my response now to even the most well-intentioned stranger who asks about my height or my shoe size or how the weather feels way up here. After nearly 50 years, I no longer feel obliged to respond to such questions. So, to that extent, I am more confident and psychologically resilient than I was as a child giant navigating the streets of Manchester and the expressions of fear, shock, and ridicule that met me at every turn.

I am still evolving, however. In professional settings, I still feel compelled to disarm the reactions to my size. This colossal vessel that contains my brain is, at best, a distraction. Audiences are never sure what to make of me, and their cognitive dissonance only worsens once they hear me speak. British people fully expect an American accent. And Americans tend to assume that all Brits look like the Queen or Harry Styles. So everything about me is out of sorts.

Thus, I lead with credentials. I wear my CV like a sandwich board and overdress for most occasions. I seek to impress by appending that haughty "OBE" to my name (which isn't even my real name because using my real name would likely have the opposite effect—but we'll get to that).

I list my qualifications as instinctively as clearing my throat. A preemptive and defensive measure employed to shake loose false perceptions. To convince skeptics that what they're seeing is more than a giant ex-jock who clearly spends more time these days eating airport and hotel food than running wind sprints.

Neutralizing people's impressions is not easy; words are not always enough. Several years after I retired from basketball, I was seated on a flight from London to Boston and a flight attendant approached before takeoff to ask what team I played for. She framed her question in the present tense, despite the fact that I was already graying in the beard and significantly rounder than the average pro athlete. It was flattering in a way but also a bit daft.

"I don't play basketball," I replied. "I'm a psychologist."

That response appeared to break her brain for a moment. At the least, it caught her off guard. She nodded her head and furrowed her brow suspiciously, and then gave an exaggerated "Hmmm" before returning to her work, as if to say, "You're pulling my leg, but this plane is about to take off so we'll revisit the matter later."

And sure enough, we did. She returned with a colleague once we leveled. They had sorted the mystery apparently, saying, "We know, we know. You play for the Boston Celtics."

This was not true and never has been true. For those of you who didn't follow my NBA career, between the years of 1995 and 2005, I set the league on fire and was widely regarded as the UK's version of Michael Jordan. For those of you who *did* follow my career or even watched me play, I apologize. And I ask that you please not talk to those other people.

In any case, I played for three different teams, but the Celtics were not among them.

"I don't play for the Celtics, no," I said. "I don't play at all anymore. I'm a psychologist."

This either didn't compute or they weren't buying it. There were sheepish smiles and nervous nods. It was easy for them to envision me as a professional athlete, even with the gray and the excess pounds. They could not as easily envision me as a psychologist, however. Even after I said, earnestly and directly, that I was a psychologist.

They eventually accepted that I was not an active player. But I'm not sure the psychologist part broke through. They could maybe accept that I was an ex-pro with a hobbyist's fancy for psychology. That's reasonable and even kind of adorable. But an *actual* psychologist seemed a bridge too far.

I don't share this to air grievances or to bemoan the crosses I bear. Mine has been a full and varied life. But every day of it that I can remember has been lived as a giant. And that never goes away. The impact of being a giant does not diminish with time. It factors into my every decision. It influences the way people see me and the way that I interact with them.

People never get used to giants. We're always new and curious and inviting of strange behavior. As you might expect, at night about town, being a giant intersects with my Blackness in a way that frightens people, causing them to cross the street or pull their children close. But, conversely, in controlled environments, I find my size attracts people—people who are not necessarily seeking notice or engagement but, rather, protection or security of some sort. In shops or in conferences, people collect and linger near me with no apparent intent. It's as if they've been drawn into the lee of a vast reef—a safe harbor should trouble arise.

As a giant, I approach the world from a radically different perspective. When I shake your hand, it's a handshake measured for you, specifically. It is not for someone of your gender or age or stature. It is custom delivered because, for giants, there is a fine but critical line between "Ah, that's a nice, butch handshake" and "Ah, my hand is now sausage meat, thank you."

Like Superman, I treat the world as if it's made of cardboard so that I don't accidentally tear it. If someone asks for directions to the loo, I can't thoughtlessly pivot and point. Because if someone is lurking in one of my blind spots and we make contact, that someone will likely die. Even in our everyday behavior, giants must be mindful of the disproportionate space we occupy and the power we wield. Everything we do is magnified, every interaction meaningful.

The Promises of Giants requires you to recognize that you, too, are a giant. Some of you may be a giant to fewer people, and some of you may be larger giants than others. But everyone is a giant to someone or has the potential to be.

It's hard to recognize this when you're tiny, which from my perspective most of you are! From my elevated view, I can see you all bouncing off each other in crowded spaces. It brings me back to high school science, where we would observe smoke particles through a microscope as they ricocheted off each other and the surrounding molecules of air. That's how you look: Brownian motion in human form. Tiny people buzzing around on their phones, earbuds in, scrambling past each other. Turning corners, nearly avoiding collisions. "Oops, sorry, pardon me." There is incidental contact, but no damage done. At worst, a bit of coffee is spilled.

That's because most of your tiny bodies could be stored in an overhead bin. They generally do not put you at risk of causing unintentional physical harm. They do not require you to be ever cognizant of the space that you occupy. And, as a result, they make it easy for you to underestimate the influence you wield. Being tiny fosters a certain laziness that allows you to forget that, in some contexts of your life, you're every bit the giant that I am.

Forgetting that you're a giant—even for a moment—can have dire consequences. Several years ago I spent the New Year holiday in Manchester with my sister Muriel and some of her friends. We ended up at a nightclub on Canal Street, the heart of Manchester's "gay village," and Muriel's crew immediately took to the dance floor. I stayed behind, ever the wallflower. I'm not good at dancing "like no one's watching," but neither of my sisters feel such restraint or inhibition. They dance with a graceful confidence and abandon that I envy, and on this night Muriel owned the floor. She was on fire. The entire club was, really. It was brilliant.

For me, it had been a challenging and lonely year. But standing there, I could see it all melting away. An unpleasant chapter giving way to better days ahead. The crowd's energy steadily rose with the approach of midnight, and it felt like I was shedding a skin. Experiencing my own personal revival.

At the height of this, with just minutes left in the year, the DJ broke out "Can You Feel It," an absolute banger by the Jackson Five. No song was more likely to send me to the dance floor than "Can You Feel It." So when I heard those opening beats pulse through the club, I went for it.

There was a beautiful urgency to the moment—my sister and her friends elated to have me join them, the crescendos in the music, the carefree mass of bodies joyfully bouncing and boogying into a new year of fresh possibility. It was cathartic to be among them. To lose myself in the mob and let go of self-consciousness. In no time, I had worked up a sweat, and as far as giant, awkward dancing goes, I was pretty good! Or at least committed. In for a penny, in for a pound—it was my dance floor now! Step aside, Muriel!

It felt like I hadn't been dancing for more than a few seconds before I felt my sister tugging at me from behind and punching my shoulder. Her cheerfulness was gone, replaced by something like fear or fury. She was yelling, but I couldn't make out her words over the blasting music. She kept punching and dragging me, eventually pointing to a small huddle of people on the other side of the club who were no longer dancing. Looking closer, I realized there was a man kneeling amid them with blood gushing from a misshapen nose that sat half an inch or so to the left of where it should have been. Muriel shot me a glare and pointed emphatically, and it dawned on me that I was somehow responsible for the state of this man's broken face. I checked my elbows and forearms for blood or any evidence of the blow, but there was nothing. Not even a spot. It seemed impossible that I could inflict such damage without noticing, but there was no denying it. I had smashed this man's nose to bits.

TEN! ... NINE! ... EIGHT!

As I pieced together the horror of what I'd done, the DJ started the countdown to the new year. Exquisite timing!

SEVEN! ... SIX! ... FIVE!

I pushed through the crowd to apologize but was intercepted by the man's friends, who didn't want any more trouble. Their clothes were wet with blood. I insisted that I'd meant no harm, and I begged to be of some assistance, but they were not interested in my compassion or aid. They had their friend on his feet now and were focused on getting out of the club as swiftly as possible.

FOUR! ... THREE! ... TWO!

I screamed over their heads to my victim, "I'm so sorry, it was an accident! I didn't mean it!" Whether he heard me or not, I have no idea. But as they escorted him away, he turned and met my eyes with a cold and vacant stare that lasted only a second but stayed with me forever. My remorse and my intentions—or lack thereof—meant nothing in the face of what my actions had done to his face.

ONE!!! ... HAPPY NEW YEAR!!!

I wish that I could sear the image of that sad and expressionless gaze into the minds of every parent, teacher, "cool kid," coach, and manager who takes for granted their own power. Because of me, this man and his friends would spend the first hours of 1998 in an emergency room. I had forgotten that I was a giant. I'd allowed myself to "let loose," which is perfectly acceptable. But I can't "let loose" with the same disregard as everyone else. In fact, I can't do *anything* in the same way as everyone else. And when it comes to our interactions with others; neither can you.

Giants play by different rules. "Letting your hair down" does not apply when the hair is on the head of a giant. Everything we do and say—everything connected to us—is magnified, scrutinized, interpreted, and obsessed over. Every casual interaction walking to the break room, every punctuation decision in an email, every tweak of your face during a video call. With nothing more than a glance, you can make or ruin someone's entire day. And the higher you ascend, the more this is true. Actions that could pass unnoticed early in your career have seismic implications when you're a giant.

Our words as giants amplify and echo and carry the capacity to inspire or destroy. Nothing we do is ordinary. And there are no "breaks" from being a giant. You can't shatter someone's nose and then excuse it away because your mind was in another place. Giants don't get to pick their spots.

We wish it were otherwise. As a giant child, I fantasized about the "Drink Me" potion and "Eat Me" cake concocted by Charles Lutwidge Dodgson, writing as Lewis Carroll, in *Alice's Adventures in Wonderland*. In truth, I fantasized about all types of cake back then. But this cake in particular, paired with the potion, allowed its consumer to be a giant only when it served them and to shrink when they wanted to go unnoticed or retreat from sight altogether.

Such shapeshifting is never that easy, though plenty of leaders delude themselves to think otherwise. They eat the cake before delivering good news or soaking in the glow of praise that is perhaps due also to those left in their shadow. But when things get bumpy or they want to blend in and "let loose," they drink the potion. They drink it when they feel too busy to expend energy on personal exchanges. They operate under the false illusion that, fueled by an endless supply of potion and cake, they can move fluidly from kingmaker to rank-and-file and back again. But the truth is, that just can't be done.

You can't be a "conditional" giant. It would be brilliant if you could, because being a giant has obvious advantages. The appearance of having power alone feels pretty great for most people. The fact that this appearance is often accompanied by higher salaries, prestigious titles, and increased resources? All the better.

But, as Uncle Ben warned, with great power comes great responsibility. The onus of being a giant is unyielding. It requires vigilance from the second you begin your morning commute. We are predisposed to believe in pivotal moments—the idea that we will be able to predict and prepare for the most significant events and interactions. We'll see these moments as they approach at a measured pace. Some will even be booked in our calendars well in advance. And because we were ready and recognized the importance of the moment, we will handle it with aplomb, give a textbook response—we'll be amazing.

But that's bunkum. That's not how it works. The most lasting interactions are seldom planned, and you will rarely know which will be the most consequential. Think about your own life and career, and you'll see that this is true. When we reflect on mentors or managers who've inspired and shaped us, we rarely think first of their performance in formal or familiar situations—the sales meeting speech or the annual performance review. We remember how they treated us in everyday moments or unexpected periods of strife.

The ethos of *The Promises of Giants* is to approach each moment like it's pivotal and acknowledge that we cannot prepare for the moment of impact because we will rarely see it coming. If you cannot embrace that and start thinking like a giant, the rest of this book will be useless. Because the underlying premise to the Promise is an acceptance that you are—by virtue of your title, your expertise, your experience, or your network—a disproportionately powerful entity. Indeed, a giant. And more is required from giants than what is covered by codes of conduct or performance objectives.

Giants will always set the tone, but giants should never dominate. In most workplaces, it is the preferred style of named leaders that shapes the dynamic of their relationships with direct reports and the broader workforce. In the Promise model, leaders must tailor their style during every interaction—planned or spontaneous—to engage that specific individual in that specific space and time.

The Promises of Giants guarantee a certain type of lived experience under the umbrella of that leader. It is an assurance that we will view people as just that—people. Complicated beings, not interchangeable bots on an assembly line. The "who" of them will never be incidental. We commit to recognizing and preserving their differences and idiosyncrasies not as a diversity check-box exercise but as a strategy for winning. Embracing people fully allows them to arrive at work each day with every available asset focused on collective goals and no parts shrouded by doubt or the fear of disclosure.

But it's not a one-way street; we're not offering a free or easy ride. Conscientious, effective leadership involves a quid pro quo of sorts. As leaders, we make an immutable promise and set the standard for an enduring lived experience. In return, we can expect our people to commit wholly to the work and to their colleagues—to share credit and blame as appropriate, to disagree constructively, to provide managers critical feedback, and to perform to their peak ability. We can expect all of this, but only if we are providing compassionate, consistent, and clear direction.

Leadership is a promise to support people not only through the inherent demands of work but also through the unique challenges that we put forward to stretch and develop them. Whether they meet those demands and challenges is not determined by output alone. As leaders, we promise to assess effort, process, diligence, and the individual's willingness to learn, adapt, and grow into a true colleague and, in time, a fellow custodian of the culture.

The Promises of Giants is, as its title suggests, a collection of promises. Some are made to the people you work with most intimately, and others are made to your workplace as a whole. But we start with the promises that you make to yourself alone.

None of the promises are just *about* you—even that first group. Those promises are directed *to* you, yes. But leadership is never about the needs or desires of the leader or the external pressures that influence that leader. Leadership is not about the leader at all, in fact. It's about the people that leaders elevate and inspire and those that they leave bloodied on the dance floor.

Throughout this text, I refer to "leaders." But leadership is not the exclusive domain of people managers or high-level executives. Leadership can be demonstrated from any level of any organization. It's accessible to anyone who is willing to invest effort and emotional energy. Anyone who is willing to take a proactive role in maximizing their influence and shaping the world around them. Because on their own, the promises of leadership are neither profound nor difficult to grasp. They ask for nothing that exceeds your capability. But they are promises that have an enormous impact when kept by giants. And a devastating impact when broken.

When I was a boy, my mother shared an African proverb that said, "When an axe meets wood, only the axe forgets." These are useful words to bear in mind as you travel through this book and embrace your new life as a giant. We could spend time arguing about whether you're the biggest or the smallest axe, but fundamentally that's time wasted—an indulgence to avoid considering that even a tiny axe can fell a tree—and that, consequentially, we all have a responsibility to act with vigilance and care.

CHAPTER 1

I Promise to View Myself Critically, But Not Cruelly

When was the last time you were lost? Truly lost, wondering, "Where in the heck am I, and how do I get where I'm going?" Pulled over in the breakdown lane lost, rifling through the road atlas you keep in the glove compartment. Or wandering through an unfamiliar neighborhood, craning your neck to make out unfamiliar names on unfamiliar street signs. That kind of lost.

I suspect it's been a while—especially if you're old enough to have experienced a physical road atlas at all! These days, you're more likely to have your head down in that situation, eyes glued to your smartphone. Keep it charged, and you will never be lost. It always shows the way.

We value our navigation apps because they direct us to wherever we want to go, using the swiftest and most efficient route. But we take for granted their true genius—the ability to, without any effort or input on our part, identify precisely where we are on this Earth. *Where am I right now?* A paper map will show all of the roads that lead to your destination. But if you don't know where you're starting from, that paper map is useless. Knowing your current location is key to routing the path forward.

Likewise, knowing yourself intimately and objectively is a vital first step toward realizing your potential as a person and as a leader. You cannot grow without an accurate understanding of who you are and where you're starting from, and there is no app for that. Finding your way to the best version of yourself—as an influencer, contributor, colleague, family member, friend, or leader—requires persistent effort and constant introspection. Because, while you may find yourself in familiar and comfortable surroundings today, that can change quickly. The political, cultural, and economic landscape is shifting at a pace that affects us all. Any one of us could wake up to find that our jobs and workplaces have dramatically changed or even disappeared. And if that happens to you, your ability to fully understand yourself will be integral to how you proceed.

I first learned about the power of introspection from my mother, Wendy Amaechi, who remains the greatest influence in my life. In both of her full-time roles—single mother of three and family physician with a community surgery in the north of England—she embodied *The Promises of Giants*, both in word and deed. And the lessons she shared continue to resonate with me in new and unexpected ways—little Easter eggs of wisdom and benevolence that pop into my consciousness, seemingly whenever they're needed most. It was Mum who helped chart my course to professional basketball and helped lay the foundation for my work now in the discipline of psychology.

I started playing basketball in 1987 when I was 16, developing basic skills and learning the rules on the fly during pickup at a small community college gym. While you might think it quite predictable that an enormous Black child would eventually gravitate toward sport and basketball specifically, it was not a fait accompli in my case. I was (and am) a nerd and a geek, who knew nothing about sport and cared even less. My introduction to the game was late and accidental, but it didn't take me long to recognize my potential, given my physical advantages.

I didn't love basketball per se. In fact, I never loved it and still don't. But in those first weeks in the gym, I fell in love with the way I felt around the game, being embraced by peers who praised me and believed in me and wanted me on their team. Until then, my height had been a liability and the source of isolation and embarrassment. Suddenly, though, it was an asset. It had a practical value in that it connected me to people who viewed me as special and believed in my potential for greatness. It connected me to people who would laugh with me and not at me, people who pushed me to perform and supported me through failure in a way I had never experienced before. That was the initial allure.

On my first day of practice, I learned about the NBA. Although I didn't know then what those letters stood for—National Basketball Association—I knew it was a place where I could be seen completely differently than my day-to-day experience suggested. While it was important that the NBA was a place where I could make a living playing basketball, at that time it more represented the idea of being paid to feel like I belonged—like I felt in that gym in Chorlton—rather than some path to riches in and of itself. I will admit to being seduced by the thoughts of eternal sunshine: after all, that's *all* you saw in 80s US television—sunshine and heroes— and the notion of cheering crowds rather than jeering passersby was really compelling, but I was not thinking about strangers cheering me on and wearing shirts bearing my name. As a person who spent much of their day wishing to be invisible, I thought that a modicum of fame would be a tolerable exchange for sunshine and belonging, but I never lost sight of the fact that basketball wasn't an end to itself; it would simply provide an alternative path to what I truly dreamed of as a child—financial security and a career as a psychologist.

My mother understood my early fascination with psychology and the way that people think and behave. But I left her in the dark about my burgeoning interest in basketball and the places it was taking my imagination. She knew I was spending time at the gym, but it could easily have been a passing phase and, frankly, she was probably just relieved that her lonely, chunky boy was finally exercising and alluding to "friends." How could she know that a year from college and only months after touching a ball for the first time, her bashful bookworm was scheming to play in the NBA? She didn't even know that there *was* an NBA.

I presented these intentions to Mum in a deliberate and dramatic fashion. She was lying in bed, where each night before sleep she would listen to *The Archers*, a long-running BBC radio drama about the trials and tribulations of a rural community. As I had on other occasions when there were important matters to discuss, I stood by Mum's window and gazed toward the Victorian railway viaduct that dominates my hometown, Stockport. From outside, the industrial lights of a nearby office parking lot cast an amber glow into her room, which was otherwise dark. I enjoyed this spot because the backlighting of my profile created a brooding and serious theatrical effect.

"Mum ..." I said, summoning a deep breath. "I'm not sure where I want to go to university."

She did not rush to respond; for a time the space was filled only by the sounds of sheep bleating from the radio. Eventually, she replied, though with only modest enthusiasm. "Well ... There's Manchester University."

Yes, I thought, *Manchester University. Close to home, that's fine. Let her go on.* I said nothing.

"And then there's Liverpool. And Leeds. And Birmingham."

Good yes, perfectly fine institutions. Still, I said nothing. *Let her sense my anguish through my silence—let her search for the source of consternation behind this stare.*

"There's even London. There are lots of choices in London."

Yes, London. I'm moderately terrified of the IRA bombings I keep hearing about, but yes, there's London. Go on, please.

She didn't go on. I was still at the window and didn't want to break character by shifting my gaze from the horizon. But the empty bleating of sheep was again the only sound in the room. The London offering was her last.

It is clear to me now that she was humoring me with these suggestions, buying me time to say whatever it was that I was working up the courage to say.

"But, Mother ..."

I gathered myself and pivoted toward her, pausing again for effect.

"I'm not sure what *country* I want to go to for university."

Ooh. I nailed it. The energy in the room changed immediately. Mum shifted in her bed and turned off the radio. I had her. And wait till she heard what was coming next!

"I think I'd like to go to university in America so I can play in the NBA. That's the National Basketball Association." I clarified the acronym casually as if I hadn't just learned it myself. "The NBA is where the best basketball players in the world play."

We sat with that information for what seemed like an eternity but was surely only a second or two. When Mum was sure that I'd finished speaking, she sat up, locked eyes with me, and stated quite plainly and without judgment, "That sounds challenging." Queen of the understatement she was.

"How are you going to manage that?"

I pointed to the obvious first. I was Black, I was six foot eight, and I was still growing. In my world, which extended no further than Stockport, I had never seen anyone who even approached my size. So it stood to reason that my color and height alone would put me on the fast track. I considered myself a Black unicorn, and as such I would surely be in high demand.

"I'll do a year of high school in the US first," I proposed. Even unicorns need to develop their skills, after all. And I was realistic enough to appreciate how far I was behind the competition waiting in America. But it was nothing that couldn't be overcome by a year playing at any random high school!

"Then I will get a scholarship to a top university"—as one does—"And then I'll get selected in the draft—that's what they call it, the NBA Draft—and I'll make a lot of money."

It was a watertight plan. Feeling confident, I sweetened the deal.

"And when I make it, I'll buy you a new house!" Who could argue with that?

Mum was not impressed. She was *not* impressed. But her expression betrayed nothing, one way or another. I tried not to appear overeager for a response, any response. I looked back out the window, this time toward the office park on the opposite end of the bowl of Stockport.

"Son?"

YES? WHAT? YES?!?

"Would you recognize your soul in the dark?"

Would I recognize my soul in the dark? What a thing to hear. I'd spent days orchestrating this moment and had now laid bare my ambitions, supported by a well-reasoned plan. And she asks about my soul in the dark? *What does that have to do with anything? And aren't we atheists anyway?* I'd never been so frustrated with her, but she proceeded before I could reply.

"People who want to do ordinary things," she said, "They are like sticks in the river. They get thrown in at the top, and they may get stuck for a while in some reeds. Or even temporarily washed to the banks. But eventually, all things being equal, they will make their way to the sea.

"You've chosen an extraordinary destination. And as such, you can't rely on chance or fate to wash you there. People who want to do extraordinary things … they need to be armed with full knowledge of who they are.

"Most people can't describe their true selves in enough detail that they could recognize themselves without their physical reflection. Would you recognize your soul in the dark?"

Now she had my attention. I moved to her bedside and listened enraptured as she told me about the power and, indeed, the necessity of introspection for those who plan to achieve the unconventional and extraordinary.

"Describe yourself to me," she said when she was done. "Who *are* you?"

That question should have been easy enough for a smart kid like me. I prided myself on my intellect and my studies. I spent hours lost in books and my own thoughts. And yet, I struggled to find a meaningful reply to Mum's question. I resorted to listing the most basic physical and biological descriptors (e.g., Black, tall, British, student, son, older brother), but that wasn't what she was looking for.

"Let's take away all of that," she said. "What happens if you can't use those things?"

Neither my mother back then nor I today would suggest that such basic characteristics are not vital to personal identity. But it is easy to start and end self-analysis within the territory of the safe or obvious—job title, age, country of origin, gender identity, and so forth. Focusing exclusively on these basic traits, however, sells us short. It diminishes individuality and quashes the nuance of experience. It overlooks intersectionality and our unique idiosyncrasies and limits our access to greater truths. So Mum pushed me to dig deeper. Over the next few days, she peppered me with questions. What is your most common state or mood? What happens when you experience the extremes of emotion? Under what circumstances do you feel peace, and how often does that occur? What agitates you? What inspires joy and lifts your spirits? What types of interactions do you avoid?

"It's blind spots and self-sabotage that derail most people in pursuit of the extraordinary," she would say. "Not the competition."

It was an invaluable study. I had been charting my destination and all that I'd hoped to accomplish. But, in doing so, I had put the cart before the horse; I had not performed a proper inventory of these less-examined spaces. I had not taken stock of what parts of my character might be incompatible with such lofty dreams—the inconvenient truths, for example, that I was lazy, that I loved eating pie, and that I generally avoided physical exertion at any cost.

The fact that I loved pie was not necessarily news. But Mum forced me to confront my indulgences in a serious and methodical way, particularly as they related to the plans I had for myself. The average NBA player carries about 4–8 percent body fat; mine was … higher. What was I going to do about that? Had I considered the sacrifice that would be required to get into that range? Did I have enough inner resolve to overcome the indisputable strength of my appetite? How many pies a week would I have to leave uneaten?

The fact that I was lazy was a more surprising revelation, at least to me. Less so to Mum, I suppose, but I had never considered myself to be so. It is true that, aside from those few months playing basketball, I had never been particularly active. I was bookish, though! I loved nothing more than curling up with a science-fiction novel and letting the hours pass by. And, to my mind, that love reflected nothing more than my superior intellect and passion for reading. But, upon closer scrutiny, I had to acknowledge that I loved the "curl up" part of "curl up with a book" every bit as much as the "book" part. I could be curled up and daydreaming and be perfectly content. Or curled up with the TV. Or a pie. Or the TV and a pie together.

This remains true today: I am inherently lazy. Left unchecked, my default state is to spend as little energy as possible, especially when it comes to physical exertion. I needed to understand that about myself early on because it was not in sync with my world-beating intentions. My mother challenged me to explore such detrimental qualities not to dissuade me from my dreams but to put me on guard. My appetite and my laziness were not going away and could not be ignored. So, in the service of my destiny, I would need to create enduring strategies to negate them.

I was fortunate that my mother forced me toward introspection because it is not traditionally encouraged in young people. Instead, we use standardized tests to tell them what they're good at. And, from their earliest days, we ask not what they value or who they are, but, rather, what they would like to be professionally. What do you want to *do* when you grow up? What do you want to *be* when you grow up? Perhaps we should ask *who* they want to be, not what.

If you are not open to focused introspection and you do not practice it on a routine basis, you will not be a great leader— at least not by the standards of greatness that I would suggest truly matter. To be authentic, emotionally literate, intellectually curious, adaptable, and connected and engaged with those around you, introspection cannot be ignored. It is a whetstone that sharpens your inner voice, which must be trustworthy. For the rest of your professional life, that voice will be your primary source of feedback. Colleagues, direct reports, and managers will be sources as well. But the farther you advance, the more difficult it will become to acquire useful external feedback.

That doesn't mean you shouldn't seek insights from the people around you; you most definitely should. Share an experience with a colleague who generally comes from a different perspective—someone outside of your immediate peer group—and ask how she or he might have handled it. Find someone you can lean on as a "reverse mentor" of sorts—a less experienced team member or even a direct report who can provide feedback on specific areas of concern. Schedule periodic 15-minute check-ins, and be candid about what you need from them. Explain frankly, "My aspiration is to be an incredible leader. Where am I in that pursuit? I know that I have flaws. But where do they manifest, and how can I change that?"

That takes some chutzpah because you may be told stuff that won't always be pleasant. But your colleagues won't tell you everything. And they'll sometimes tell you things that aren't necessarily accurate, for better or worse. So this first promise is imperative: *to view yourself critically, objectively, and compassionately.* This means an honest, ongoing pragmatic self-assessment of strengths and weaknesses. Without an accurate understanding of your flaws and fortes, the starting point of your journey forward will be unclear, immediately setting you off course.

Many of us have known people who are unable to see their flaws, even when they're painfully obvious, self-destructive, and toxic to others. Stubborn and/or delusional, these people treat every quality or near-skill as supreme and fully matured. Some of them may be well-intended, while others are blowhards convinced that they're the cat's pajamas. You simply can't tell them anything to the contrary. But they're actually a minority.

More common are the gratuitously self-flagellant, who are hyperbolic in their self-criticism and incapable of recognizing the magnitude of their strengths and accomplishments. Many of us struggle to appreciate the qualities that can't be easily quantified in the P&L or celebrated by awards for hitting concrete targets. We're dismissive of personal triumphs that seem irrelevant to the workplace but actually have salient applications. For example, if you're a woman who is entering the workplace later in life because you were a mature student raising a family while working through school, that alone should resonate as a remarkable and relevant achievement. If it doesn't—if you can't recognize and honor the tenacity and initiative you've demonstrated to get to that point—then that can be as limiting and damaging as being an overconfident blowhard.

Selling ourselves short is an unfortunate but predictable outcome of corporate culture. "Imposter syndrome"—the feeling that you are a fraud and undeserving of your place, that you're actually substandard, and that, at any second, people will "find out" and "expose" you—has been widely discussed. But it is often framed as an individual pathology, which it is not. It is not an affliction of the meek or an absence of assertiveness; rather, imposter syndrome is a natural response to systemic waves of pressure that are pervasive in most workplaces and, indeed, throughout society. Waves of pressure that strike some people as turbulence become the wind beneath the wings of others.

The style of leadership favored by an organization is set from the top. And "the top" has traditionally been inhabited by a homogenous brand of leader. They are mostly white and mostly straight, yes. But it is more than that. Regardless of demographics, traditional leaders are largely autocratic, dominant in their relationships, and fixed in their thinking. This style is not lost on people working within organizations, who will automatically feel some sense of imposter syndrome if they cannot relate to or match the examples at the top. *I will never look like that leader or be stylistically similar*, they surmise, *so I'm essentially a pretender to a throne I could never rightly assume.*

The damage inflicted by imposter syndrome is compounded because it filters out the people we need most in leadership positions—people who are truly conscientious and concerned about delivering for both their employer and employees—often at the most critical time in their careers. If those people are not adequately supported during early leadership opportunities, they will be more prone to fall victim to imposter syndrome. And, as they retreat from leadership, the void will be filled by peers who are less troubled by feeling like a fraud so long as they advance. Those peers are less likely to be inhibited by imposter syndrome because they are empowered to believe that being a boss is their natural destiny. They may not even be concerned with managing effectively or giving appraisals or connecting with their people. Because simply by reflecting the general characteristics of the leaders at the top, they have already checked the most important box. And from there, the system is designed to accommodate their ascension.

If you do *not* check that box, you will be more susceptible to imposter syndrome. If you are a woman or a racial minority or if you are LGBTQ+, it will be more difficult to relate to high-level leadership in most workplaces. But this can also be true for introverted straight, white males, who find themselves in the shadows of charismatic, larger-than-life leaders. *How could I thrive in this space*, they naturally wonder. *I am quiet and considered, and everybody who leads here is gregarious and seemingly comfortable speaking before thousands.*

How can you be confident in your ability to lead if you don't fit into one of the classical leadership archetypes? What if you're not a zany Richard Branson type? Or a terrifying and brilliant Steve Jobs type? Or, God forbid, a terrorizing and simple Donald Trump type? We know that, like the workplace, society at large takes cues from the dominant leadership style. A week into Donald Trump's presidency, and it was nearly impossible to imagine a time when someone with the characteristics of a Barack Obama could have ever held office. Even those who opposed Trump felt compelled to adopt his tone and his tactics.

Everyone, and especially those who've never felt it, bears a responsibility to limit the damage done by imposter syndrome. It creates leaders who are overly self-critical and unable to recognize the bits that make them good. They are constantly beating themselves up and obsessing over perceived shortcomings, and that makes them neurotic, which has the unfortunate effect of making the people around them neurotic. When the person who is supposed to be leading is saying they aren't any good or showing as much through their body language, it does little to inspire confidence.

Imposter syndrome impairs judgment. Its howls of self-doubt are unnerving, and they don't just scream that you're terrible at your job. They scream that you're a fraud. That it's bad enough that you're incapable, but you're also pretending to *be* capable. It turns people who might otherwise be fine contributors as leaders or otherwise into people who are floundering, timid, and fearful. They recoil from critical decisions and challenging conversations and any situation that might expose them, which is practically every situation in high-performance scenarios. Whether it's onboarding someone new, addressing underperformance, or assessing who gets a promotion, these moments inspire fear because they threaten to expose. Imposter syndrome encourages withdrawal from those moments or avoidance altogether.

Essentially, imposter syndrome is a nasty voice in your head that sends distorted feedback. And if you lack an acute understanding of yourself, you will not know what to make of it. You will not have a perspective that allows you to separate the truth from fiction. In 2015, the Republican US Senator Jim Inhofe famously brought a snowball to the Senate floor to counter the global warming "hysteria" being pushed by "eggheads" in labs. *There is no global warming*, he argued. *This snowball is evidence.* And, indeed, a snowball is a reasonable piece of evidence if you are a person who doesn't understand the difference between climate change and weather. But if you *do* possess that basic awareness— the fundamental insight that climate is not weather—then that snowball is just a ridiculous stunt. It is flawed evidence that should be dismissed out of hand, and yet without the counter of scrutiny and knowledge, that snowball can be effectively weaponized to great effect.

Imposter syndrome sends similarly flawed evidence. And if you don't know yourself and appreciate the breadth of your skill and experience, that evidence—absurd though it may be—will be damning. It will leave you trembling when instead it should roll off your back. *I can't possibly rise to this occasion*, you'll think, even though your own history clearly indicates otherwise. If you can access that history and identify your successes and your proven proficiencies, it becomes easier to refute that voice of doubt.

When imposter syndrome sends you tumbling and spiraling down a rabbit hole of self-doubt, there are seven useful questions to ask yourself. They comprise what I refer to as the Effective Feedback Model, a useful tool with broad applicability. The model provides a handy checklist to reference while preparing to give feedback to others. But in the context of introspection, it can hold to account any voice in your head that may be disproportionately cruel or disproportionately flattering, but in either case inaccurate. Asking yourself these seven questions will keep your bravado in check as well as your imposter syndrome.

The Effective Feedback Model

1 What is the feedback's intent?

What is its impact meant to be? Does this feedback carry an earnest intent toward improvement? Is it helping the avoidance of mistakes? If the intent of the feedback is perfunctory or nebulous, it is probably not worthwhile feedback and should be viewed with skepticism.

2 Is the feedback contextual?

Does the feedback account for the entirety of the present, past, and future landscape? Does it consider all of the factors at play and the external forces that may be beyond your control? Are you convincing yourself that you can't do something, when in fact you've already done something quite comparable, albeit in a slightly different context?

---

3 Who is benefiting from the feedback?

Is that voice saying you're a fraud actually delivering feedback for your benefit? Or does it benefit no one? Is it merely a representation of how you believe others perceive you? If there is no clear beneficiary, it is bad feedback. If the person delivering the feedback is the beneficiary, it is terrible feedback.

4 Is the feedback useful now?

Does it carry value and insight, or has its moment passed? Is it relevant and informative in the present? Or does it carry the stains of a past that have already been addressed or is no longer worth dwelling on?

5 Is the feedback real?

This fifth question seems obvious, I suppose. What is being asked here, though, is whether the feedback—the message being processed in your head—is verifiably true and accurate. Or is it based on speculation? Conjecture should not contribute to feedback.

6 Is the feedback cruel?

This is perhaps the most important of the seven questions, I feel. Is the feedback in question unintentionally cruel? Or unkind by design? Because, if the voice or nature of the feedback is cruel, then it is unlikely to be good feedback. You can give effective feedback that isn't what people want to hear. You can grow from feedback that is even painful to hear. But no one improves from feedback that is cruel.

7 Is the feedback shared?

Is the opinion on which it's based shared by relevant, informed colleagues? Whether assessing yourself or others, your voice should not stand alone. Are the people around you saying they believe in you, while the voice in your head is crying out that you're crap? The feedback that reflects mainly the feelings or beliefs of one individual likely says more about that individual than it does the subject of the feedback.

We will return to this model later when we look at delivering feedback to others. But applied inwardly, the Effective Feedback Model helps us extract meaning from chaos and separate truth from fiction. Those seven questions help clarify and contextualize the messages that are constantly being sent by our inner critic. They prevent our heads from becoming echo chambers of distortion that negatively influence behavior; they encourage us to view and understand ourselves in a more complete way.

If you are averse to introspection or lack the initiative to engage in self-analysis, it will be all but impossible to fulfil *The Promises of Giants*. The force of the tide alone won't get you there. You must promise to maintain an accurate and up-to-date understanding of yourself; you must promise to be objective, detailed, eloquent, and accurate in your praise and criticism.

The journey of self-analysis that began with Mum continued beyond her death, which unbeknown to us at the time was only a few years away. It continued beyond my goals of reaching the NBA and becoming a psychologist and starting my own firm, and it will continue until my final breaths. And for this I am grateful because it is joyful work! While demanding, introspection should not feel like a burden or repetitious drudgery. It is like rereading a familiar book and discovering a new insight or turn of phrase on a page you thought you knew down to the word.

Finding your soul in the dark is not a discrete exercise. It is the essential pursuit of a lifetime, and it begins now so get started!

Activity: Soul in the Dark

Could you describe yourself in a way that you and others could recognize uniquely as you, if others couldn't see your physical form or glean your identity from your relationships to people or institutions?

Without labels describing your demographics or reference to your identity (gender, sexuality, ethnicity, etc.), your occupation, and hobbies, without using relationships labels (brother, mother, etc.), and without describing yourself in comparison to people in uniquely similar circumstances or endlessly listing your likes and dislikes, could you describe yourself in a way that even just you would recognize?

The following are a list of questions that might help start you on this path. This isn't an exercise that is completed in an hour: each question will likely spark other questions and implications that arise from some of your answers.

Once you've begun to answer some of these questions, you may want to think about people who will give you their own honest thoughts on their impressions. But make sure you delve in on your own first so you aren't too influenced by any particular person as you explore who you really are.

- What is your most common state or mood?
- How do people respond when you interact with them at first? In time?
- What impacts do you have on others when around them (how they think, feel, express themselves, etc.)?
- What are some of your great qualities? List 10 at least and be specific.
- What are some of your less helpful or negative qualities? List at least 10 and be specific.
- How and how much do you interact with about the world around you? What does this mean for your approach to connecting with others? (In answering this, don't get locked into broad categories like "introvert" or "extrovert.")
- How do you work through problems and challenges—what is your process?
- What happens to you when you experience extremes of emotion?
- How do you feel when you are at peace? How often does it happen?
- What allows you to feel most at peace?

- What factors and experiences make you uncomfortable and stressed?
- How do you respond to stress?
- How do you experience joy?
- How do you respond to feedback, compliments, and insults?
- What are your core tenants, the principles you live by? If you were to write a set of personal values, what would be the top five?
- How congruently and consistently do you live your values?
- What are your blind spots? Describe the interactions and situations that have tripped you up in the past.
- What situations have made you feel disappointed in yourself—what themes are there, if any?

There are many more questions you can ask, so don't be afraid to "follow the rabbit" and chase any answers that lead to more and different questions.

CHAPTER 2

I Promise to Commit Fully to Success

It is hard to write about winning without appearing a monster, or indeed a hypocrite. We so often see "winners" who are cruel or objectionable, just because they can be. And, in my own case, I have, when giving speeches, talked about wanting to beat my competition so soundly that they can't compete with my organization in the future … I've said that, and I still mean it. However, this is not me invoking a plague on all my competition's houses, but an invocation to myself—to be so compelling, so well-equipped, and so diligent in my work, that my organization is at least first among equals.

In the vast majority of circumstances, success in life does *not* have to have a body count.

It may seem self-evident that you are committed to winning. You are reading a book that is about achieving personal, inter-personal, and organizational success, after all. And reading takes time. And time is a commitment. Logically, if you are reading this book, you have already made a commitment to winning.

To be clear, success and "winning" within the context of *The Promises of Giants* are defined just by the fulsome achievement of one's goals—hopefully, goals of noble intent, but, if not that, at least goals designed not to harm others.

Winning is a big-picture operation for me—it's about a commitment to a vivid, long-term personal and organizational goal with a clear and unequivocal understanding of what success looks like when it happens.

When it comes to winning, I am also clear on these seven things:

1. "Nice [pleasant, thoughtful, conscientious, ethical, fair, honest, etc.] guys" don't necessarily finish last.

2. Success doesn't require cruelty.

3. Success is relative.

4. Success requires a clear, vivid and explicit vision.

5. Success requires compromise.

6. Success isn't a zero-sum game—you don't have to seek to destroy others to achieve success yourself.

7. Success hinges on the minutiae (people often think there are pivotal moments).

In this chapter, we'll look at each of these propositions in turn.

1 "Nice guys" don't necessarily finish last

People think—perhaps because of the number of complete dicks who seem to occupy positions of prestige and power—that simply by being a dick, you are more likely to win. The not-quite syllogism here is:

- All successful people are unpleasant dicks.

- All underachievers are "nice."

- Therefore, being a dick is an (undefined) performance enhancer.

It's not that you have to be warm or pleasant or soft, but you don't have to be a dick. The license to be a dick is out there because people think it's somehow connected to winning—but there is no such connection …

People think nice guys finish last. Nice guys without a plan, without technical skills, without leadership, without allies ... yes, they do finish last. But so do dickheads without a plan; these people lose, too. What's more, it's harder for them to find and maintain colleagues, not to mention get fulsome contributions to their strategy.

I think I need to say a bit more about the word "nice." I should probably say at the outset that I'm not a fan.

As you progress through this book and consider the suggestions and ideas it sets out, there will be a temptation to nod your head and think, "Yes, that is a nice idea, I'll try that. It's so nice."

So, for example, I might suggest that, when you're seated at work and someone approaches you to chat or ask a question, you need to swivel your chair *fully* in their direction. On a virtual call, it's different, but even when looking at your computer, it makes a difference if you actually look at the space the person occupies and not just deadpan at the screen. Success requires an authentic engagement with your peers, and that means a full swivel or that head movement that shows you are responding to them as an individual. Not a half-swivel or the blank stare that allows you to press through the conversation while still working on that email or excel spreadsheet in front of you. A full, all-the-way swivel.

You might read that and think, "Yes, that is *such* good advice. It could make a real difference if we all made an extra effort to fully connect with each other, undistracted. Swivel the chair all the way, that's nice. I like that. This nice gentle giant who wants us to be nice to each other has some *really* nice ideas about being really nice. We *should* be nice."

No, no, dear reader. Let's nip any such notion in the bud immediately. "Nice" as both word and concept has little value where success is at play.

My mother wouldn't let me use the word "nice." She told her children that, if intended in a favorable way, based on someone else's positive act, it could and should be replaced by a more thoughtful, descriptive and meaningful word, given even a nanosecond's thought. If somebody has done something genuinely warm and good and the best that you can muster is "nice," you've misunderstood what they've done or you're indicating that what they've done has failed to produce their intended result or is just not very important to you.

During the holidays, certainly where adults are concerned, when a gift elicits the words "Thank you—this is nice," you can almost guarantee that this means, "This gift is meaningless to me. I will rewrap it when you leave and give it to someone I care or know equally little about."

More commonly, "nice" is deployed as a Trojan horse word— one delivered to both suppress and express something inconsistent with the word's literal meaning. When not being applied as a lazy compliment, "nice" generally carries with it some sense of contempt, disappointment, mockery, or dismissiveness.

We have no shortage of these Trojan horse words, and they've become easy to recognize. For example, if someone casually says "by the way" or "one more thing," you can expect to hear what is, in fact, the most important thing—the thing that you didn't even know was a thing when you were talking about all those other things only moments ago.

"Interesting"? That means not interesting.

"I'll give it some thought" means "Thank you, but I've already given it some thought and I know the answer."

And perhaps the most obvious yet pervasive of all is "With all due respect." Nobody's fooled by that one anymore. You can smile sweetly or give an earnest furrow of the brow. But we all know "With all due respect" means roughly: "With all of the disrespect I can possibly muster while maintaining civility toward a moron of the highest order like you."

"Nice" is how you might politely respond after opening a gift from someone who doesn't know you as well as you thought or, worse, clearly holds you in the highest contempt. It's damning with faint praise. It's how you would reluctantly and generically describe someone you'd rather not trash in public. It's cheery, yet it can also be used to imply, "Let's wrap this up now and move on, shall we?" Nice.

More importantly, there's not one piece of research that I have ever read that connects the superficiality of "nice" to productivity, performance, or any other important metric related to success.

So I propose that we eradicate "nice" from our language altogether, not only because of its banality but because it is superficial and thus expendable. During challenging times, "nice" is the fat that gets cut. Initiatives and priorities that are considered only "nice to have" find a nice spot on the "nice to have" list. And we know what happens to that list the moment disruption hits: "nice to have" goes right out the window.

The reality of these modern times, of course, is that disruption is now ongoing. It is one long hit. Industries are transforming, the rules and norms are shifting, unexpected competitors are emerging, and social and political instability is palpable ... and as we have seen, global crises like pandemics can also threaten our physical and mental health.

In this environment, anything "nice to have" will sit in the waiting room twiddling its thumbs until the end of time. In a crisis, there's only enough oxygen for what is essential.

So if swiveling your chair is considered "nice," a harmless side benefit of negligible value, no one's going to do it.

I'm telling you to swivel the chair because it's the type of human action that is essential for winning in any context. And this will be true when we discuss inclusiveness or collaboration or the value of mindfulness. If these topics bring to mind finger cymbals or wellness gurus or sitting in a circle cross-legged, please knock that on the head right now. None of this is about "nice" for the sake of being "nice"; it's only about winning—making yourself and the people that surround you the absolute best they can be. *The Promises of Giants* are twenty-first-century *performance* prerogatives – precursors and essential elements for individual and organizational success in this new, disrupted landscape.

I am not a warm and fuzzy psychologist. And if you follow my Twitter feed, you'll quickly be disabused of any notion that I'm "nice." I have no tolerance for ignorance or trolls. One of my longstanding and recurring pinned tweets is: "In a world where obvious lies are transformed into public truths by the ignorant asserting their 'right to an opinion,' we must remember and insist that holding up opinions as facts is far more arrogant than asserting the primacy of facts over opinions."

Nowadays, when stupidity and bigotry rear their head, I'm unable to turn a cheek. I am there with a swift "block." I'm compelled to expose and eviscerate disinformation and nonsense and those who promote it because of the self-evident damage that the spread of disinformation is doing to the world.

Nice is banal, it's casual and it's inauthentic, and success isn't built on that wishy-washy foundation.

2 Success doesn't require cruelty

Success doesn't require cruelty. Success doesn't require cruelty. Success doesn't require cruelty.

I feel as though this needs to be a mantra.

Success doesn't require cruelty and isn't enhanced by it. You don't need to be a monster to be successful, and being successful doesn't turn people into monsters—it simply reveals that latent potential, a disregard for human decency and often just a lack of effort.

This does not mean that people will not be or feel hurt or set back by difficult conversations or challenging decisions; it means that one doesn't have to *aim* to harm people or recklessly disregard the impact of decisions on individuals. At a later point, we will talk about feedback, and we often think that critical feedback must be cruel when the opposite is true.

It isn't feedback if it's cruel.

It can hurt to hear even the most thoughtful critique, but it need not be cruel and, if it is, that's a choice—either to be thoughtless in one's preparation or to be malicious in intent.

3 Success is relative

Success for you needs to be enduringly meaningful *to you*. Most of the amazing entrepreneurial achievements of today were scoffed at before they proved themselves, and there are people who have achieved magnificent success in their own image but who may never be recognized as luminaries by the outside world.

But this narrative about a singular definition of extraordinary always being the benchmark misses the point—a life where success and winning can be a sequence of deeply purposeful and world-enhancing targets that brings you—and those in your sphere of influence—joy.

Each of you has a life with varying types and levels of privilege and advantage, and some of us have physical, psychological, and emotional (as well as geographic, sociopolitical, and economic) characteristics, that will mean that what we see as success will be different than everyone else. These are differences that will make like-for-like comparisons useless for understanding the distance traveled to achieve.

Do not tie your assessment of winning or success to someone else's mast. Create that picture of success *for you*, based on *your* context. Make it challenging, by all means. Improbable? Absolutely! Just don't make it someone else's dream. It's hard enough to achieve your own success in this world—don't make it harder and less rewarding by making your achievement someone else's.

4 Success requires a clear, vivid, and explicit vision

A clear, vivid, and explicit vision of success for you is essential.

At the personal level, perhaps it's identifying and defeating unhealthy habits, increasing your effectiveness as a teammate in the truest sense of the word, or setting out to develop a set of skills or competencies to get yourself your dream job.

At the organizational level, this may be measured by profit and loss, but that more often than not is related to the levels of employee engagement, quality of experience, and so many more of the human factors that underpin sustainable organizational performance.

While it's important to pick a valid target, whatever it may be, you must promise to commit fully to that success. Because winning by this definition is the driving motivation behind all that's encompassed in *The Promises of Giants*.

Just know this: if your target is a tangible element or even a number and the achievement of that number will be a challenge, then you are going to need more than a number to achieve it.

In science fiction, there is the concept of a "future history"— whereby the pictures sci-fi authors paint with words make it seem like they must have visited the future in order to write about it so completely and compellingly. We'll talk about this in a later chapter and how you can create an irresistible picture of your future that can help drive you toward success when the doldrums of discipline and exhaustion set in.

5 Success requires compromise

This might be the hardest lesson I've learned.

In my day job, winning means compromise. I've missed the boat on this particular lesson before.

Several years ago, my colleagues and I built a very expensive digital learning platform for incorporating inclusive behaviors and understanding into everyday action in the workplace.

Aside from the usual early bugs and glitches, it really was remarkable. It followed the rules of pedagogy (how to teach and how people learn), it was multimedia, interactive, colorful, contextual (we understood our clients' workplaces), and yes, it was even fun. It was everything I could hope for, eliminating the drudgery of "click and quiz."

But guess what?

No one wanted it. We built an ideal, and people didn't want that. They wanted something less ambitious, more compliance-based, and much, much less time-consuming, and instead, we had tried to eat the whole elephant in one bite. No matter how successful our platform was in execution, we had forgotten that our appetite is not the bellwether for *all* appetites!

Now I know better, I know that the introduction of an imperfect but sound intervention as part of a slow but strategic approach can get the results, even if those early interventions pain me because they are neither as effective nor as enjoyable as I would prefer.

One of my many flaws is that I love to be right. I love people to know I'm right, and I spend a *lot* of time around people whose insights challenge and inform me so I can be (more often than not), right.

But now I know we are in a long game—I'm not clear that it's infinite, but it's long. So every single day, I ask myself one question as I engage with myopic people, intransigent challenges, or difficult decisions.

"Do I want to win, or do I want to be right?"

To be clear, this actually means:

"Do I want to win (in the long game), or do I want to be right (right now)?" The question is so ingrained in my language and that of my team that we can use the shorthand version as we challenge our thinking.

I talk a lot with coaching clients who are looking to progress. It's common for these high achievers to have most, if not all, of the technical skills required for progression, but be missing this key question.

I think everyone should understand two things in the context of this compromise: capital and crow.

Each of us needs to understand how to amass interpersonal and reputational capital, the intangible asset that grants us leeway to influence a decision or operate against conventions and norms.

You need to understand how to earn it, how to maintain its usefulness, how to recognize when it might expire, and how and when to use it judiciously.

Additionally, we need to understand when it's time to "eat crow." We need to understand that one doesn't just "eat crow" when we've made a mistake (you know—those moments you bite your tongue or take unearned blame without rebuttal); we can do so strategically—biting our tongue when the opportunity to be right meets a consequence we'd rather avoid. Or supporting a subpar strategy or approach because we can see an opportunity to enhance it later rather than creating a futile challenge at that moment, that might leave us forever sidelined.

Even as I write these words, they begin to sound Machiavellian, but I don't think it has to be so cynical in practice. I simply maintain that entering an environment where everyone is playing chess and attempting to play checkers is likely a road to nowhere.

Of course, there are personal principles we should never violate. Luckily, for most of us, we are not regularly confronted by those moments. But even where decisions may seem stark, there may still be compromises for most of us. Internal conditions, like having dependents who rely on you for income and external conditions, like debt or a crashing economy will impact the true scope of your options. These and other factors will make the question "Do I want to win (in the long game) or do I want to be right (right now)?" even more important. It is an unsatisfying truth that—for most us—our world is an eternal compromise.

6 Success isn't a zero-sum game

You don't have to seek to destroy others to achieve success yourself. There are, of course, finite resources in some areas, and clearly, some job roles are in short supply or suffer an overabundance of candidates. So it can seem, on the micro-level, as if success for you, *must* mean the downfall of another.

You have been encouraged to think this way by people who know that pitting you against others who aspire has historically been the secret of everything from depressing wages to eliminating employee protections.

I think competitor analysis is important: understanding what others who might be pursuing your ideal goal are doing to enhance themselves can provide you with helpful nuggets or insights. But whether in sport or in the corporate world, controlling your controllables, learning at every stage and remaining focused on your personal excellence, is still the path to success.

7 Success hinges on the minutiae

My organization has a set of guiding behaviors—called "OB1s" (Obi-Wans), and one of them is all about the minutiae. It's a call to be eager in the face of the mundane, vexing, and obscure.

So often the tiny, seemingly inconsequential acts are overlooked, almost like people are coasting until they will be called upon for some truly consequential, Herculean task.

This labile approach is not the key to success. The idea that success is a function of a couple of significant and memorable moments is just a function of our mind latching on to a particular moment and considering it the cause of our success.

Post hoc ergo propter hoc is an informal fallacy that means "After this, therefore because of this," and it's how our brains often consider our triumphs or our failures—"If something big happened before my success/failure, it must have been the cause of my success/failure."

In all the conversations I have had with uber-successful people—from sport, politics, business, philanthropy, and the public sector—once you get past the memorable "pivotal" moments they see as significant and burrow deeper, there is a revelation around the importance of the mundane and ordinary—seemingly inconsequential—decisions and actions.

It's considerably easier to maintain a focus on the important details when you remind yourself daily that—despite what your memory tells you—there are no "pivotal moments," that enduring success is built upon equalizing attention to detail, focus, and effort across everything you do.

It's lovely to reminisce and think about those moments where "everything changed," but when forging a new path, it is more useful to consider the thoughtful and energetic placement of every step than conserve energy for the occasional future sprint.

I have my day diarized to a T. I put in almost everything I do with at least some detail in each entry to allow me to see when an outcome is achieved—and, perhaps more importantly, when a milestone is missed—and exactly what my team and I did to achieve it.

The Promises of Giants is not about "soft skills" or being nice. Many of my clients talk about winning in these extreme terms. But when the rubber meets the road, they behave in ways that make clear that they don't really intend to back up their winning rhetoric with behaviors to match. They are convinced of their commitment to winning. But, in truth, they're only committed to the extent that they can remain comfortable or completely aligned with their own worldview.

We'll explore this in greater detail later, but the type of success I'm interested in you achieving requires discomfort. It requires a natural-born pie-eater to adhere to a life without pie—delaying gratification and prioritizing long-term reward over quick and easy highs. It requires that we shrug off our natural impulse to simply survive the moment with as little discomfort as possible. It requires us every day to rise above any sense of routine or mundanity that might lull us toward complacency.

This version of success requires an appreciation for so-called marginal gains of *all* kinds—not just the external performance enhancers that require no personal graft. People are selective in their appreciation of incremental improvement. We'll obsess over a tweak to a production workflow that yields a 1 percent efficiency gain, we'll marvel at advances in training or equipment that shave fractions of a second off an athlete's time, but we'll dismiss as "nice to have" the gains that are made by simple acts like consistently giving people your full attention even when it's inconvenient or ill-timed. We take that second to pause and swivel the chair all the way, not because it pays an immediate and monstrous dividend, but because it is one slight yet meaningful long-term investment in the health of our organization.

People like marginal gains that require little personal effort; think of swimmers who wear a special suit that makes you faster or companies that put out "free" fruit in the morning to boost workers' energy. Those that mean a real investment in time and energy—for example remembering your new colleague's name because this will lead them to work harder—appear to be beyond the pale to many.

A commitment to success is a commitment to expend the required emotional and intellectual energy—and leaders are required to put in more time and energy than others. Your emotional energy is the only currency of value here. You cannot win with a reliance upon organizational investments in or changes to process and infrastructure. Those will be sporadic, slow to arrive, minimally effective, and often beyond your control.

Winning requires that you vigilantly tend to *everything* that is within your control, including all of the dusty stuff in the corners that you'd rather not deal with. It requires doing lots of things you won't want to do, spending time you won't want to spend in ways that you don't want to spend it. If you cannot commit to that, then you are not truly committed to winning. So it is questionable as to whether you should continue reading this at all. *The Promises of Giants* is not about nice, and it's not about "nice to haves." It is about winning on your own terms, challenging yourself to achieve something meaningful to you and those closest to you.

CHAPTER 3

I Promise to be Bold *and* Vulnerable

The way we frame boldness versus vulnerability will mean that they might seem strange bedfellows, but they are actually a perfect pair that both moderate and heighten each other's impact. Opening yourself up to either can seem daunting and even terrifying, but together they can be a difference-maker and I'd encourage you to embrace the possibilities that both provide.

Consider how much time has been lost throughout your life: How many opportunities have come and gone? How much energy has been spent fretting and procrastinating? How constrained have you been by anxieties and fears that proved unfounded?

When I was very young—probably six or so—my mother would take us to a playground that featured a towering slide with a steepness that to me as a child looked like a 90-degree drop. I would sit atop it agonizing over whether to let myself fall, as other kids queued behind me, restless for their turn. Time after time, this episode ended with me sheepishly retreating, paralyzed by the fear of how forcefully gravity would toss me down the slide, dare I let it.

I suspect that you can predict where the story goes from there. One day, with a little extra nudge from Mum, I worked past the fear and let myself fall—a descent that was far and away the most exhilarating thrill I'd ever known. I can recall vividly the joy and the rush of adrenaline. The immediate desire to run back to the ladder and do it again and again and again. But I also remember how quickly that joy was replaced by regret. I had wasted nearly a year—a sixth of my life!—dithering over whether I should attempt this terrifying thing that turned out to be not only *not* terrifying, but, in fact, *amazing*. And worse, I was already outgrowing the playground. The tiny window of time that I had to enjoy this thrill was closing, and I'd only just gotten started.

Most of us have had similar experiences and are familiar with the surge of emotions associated with conquering fear. We've learned that, when we demonstrate the ability to be bold, paired with the willingness to be just a little vulnerable, good things usually follow. We have all felt that relief of "Ah, that wasn't so bad after all. Lesson learned." And yet it's a lesson that often must be relearned time and again with every new context. Perhaps on the next trip up a different slide, we still hesitate. Or in the face of a new and different challenge, we're unable to access the combination of characteristics that previously propelled us.

Even equipped with the memories of dragons bested—and the knowledge that we possess the power to slay—we shy away. Because, make no mistake, it is effortful to be bold. It is difficult to be vulnerable. And for these reasons, the promise to be both will be particularly challenging to keep. But you *must*. Because being bold in the face of a challenge, and allowing yourself to be vulnerable in the face of potential loss, opens up an entire spectrum of possibilities that would not otherwise be available.

But you do need both. For many, the invitation to be bold will be more alluring than the invitation to be vulnerable. Intrinsically, boldness is conflated with courage and so has a more positive spin and is perhaps looked on with more favor than vulnerability, which is often associated with weakness or a lack of courage. But the two are a powerful combination and each far less powerful on their own.

When firefighters commit to a life filled with risk and danger, that is a bold decision. What makes them heroic, however, is their acceptance of vulnerability and their preparation to forge ahead in full knowledge of the potential risks. As humans, they understand they are flammable, and yet they know that, with preparation enabled by a pragmatic insight into their vulnerability, they can successfully charge into the blaze nonetheless.

Boldness alone is often reckless. It strives for goals that are admirable but often fanciful and perhaps even without a binding purpose; vulnerability alone is meek. It seeks to lower the bar of ambition and focus only on the readily attainable—with a guarantee of safety.

In contrast, boldness paired with vulnerability is transformative. It introduces the possibility of being wounded, whether emotionally or psychologically, career-wise or financially, while forcing our ambition to plot a path that is neither as comfortable as we might ordinarily choose, nor as irresponsible as the one our ego or partners-in-crime might goad us along.

This "middle way" does not preclude audacious ambition; it simply necessitates a suitably pragmatic plan to ameliorate foreseeable traps and hold ourselves accountable. Ultimately, it both enhances the likelihood of us meeting our goals and avails us opportunities to reach even loftier heights with a more radical upside.

Sometimes the vulnerability we must face doesn't come so much in the form of a risk of failure as in the risk of mockery when we declare what we plan to achieve—mockery based on perceptions of our own capabilities, commitment, and talent.

When I was in the League, I used to coach children at basketball camps, and at the beginning of our sessions, when we were just getting to know each other, I would ask the group, "OK now, tell me, who here wants to play in the W/NBA?"

And in every group there was one kid whose hand shot up past her or his ear and straight to the sky, a proud, knowing grin across their face, and, just as surely, a few of the other kids might chortle at them. The laughter typically came from the kids who had raised their hand halfway only to *not* appear *un*ambitious in front of friends.

But I would tell all of them then, as I tell you now, that it's not about whose hand goes up *first* as much as it's about whose hand goes up *with certainty*.

Those hands that went up like a flare, practically daring peers to mock and challenge their ambition, belonged to people who had weighed the opportunity and come away, not thinking that playing in the W/NBA is somehow easy, but that vulnerability to the mockery of peers too afraid to embrace their boldness is probably not going to be a significant obstacle to achieving their goal.

I very much enjoy that at least a handful of the hands that shot up in those days have since graced WNBA and NBA courts. I only hope that those who mocked these standouts are chastened by their peers' success in the face of personal peril and peer judgment.

I was always up front about my intentions around everything I've ever achieved, including basketball. As far-fetched as they sounded to my peers, I told anyone who would listen what I was setting out to do. In my yearbook quote, I wrote specifically that I planned to play in the NBA, win a championship, and become quite wealthy in the process.

John Amaechi

1981-1989

Address: 70 Winchester Drive
           Heaton Norris
           Stockport
           Cheshire Sk4 2NN

Ambition: To play on a NBA
           championship team
           in the States and
           earn a lot of money

My entry in my school yearbook

I look back at my decision to be so visible in my yearbook, after a life in school attempting to be invisible, in two ways. The yearbook signaled my impending exit from school, and perhaps I thought that, no matter what happened, its pages would fade to nothing and be lost to time. But with hindsight, I feel I also needed to publish my bold ambition, because, without that, there was no peril and no need for vulnerability and the impetus that could provide.

My declaration was juvenile goal setting, for sure, but, to an outsider, it must have sounded preposterous. The UK had no history of sending players to the NBA, and I showed no signs of being the first. In my most high-profile game among fellow 17-year-olds, playing in the historic Royal Albert Hall, I logged three whole minutes off the bench and posted straight zeroes across the stat sheet, save for one clumsy foul I committed.

At that point, it would have been bold to declare with any confidence that I would one day play in the British Basketball League (BBL). But doing so would not have left me vulnerable. No one would have batted an eye if I pledged in my yearbook that I'd make the BBL. Undeniably, I was tall and had raw potential. So it would have been reasonable to believe that, with some refinement, I could eventually compete in the far inferior pro league of my homeland.

I wanted more, though. Once I learned about the NBA, it became *the* destination and I grew progressively obsessed with getting there. International television coverage was scarce back then, reserved for only the biggest games, which always featured the Boston Celtics and Los Angeles Lakers. Although I had lived in the States only briefly as a child before moving to the UK, I was born in Boston, Massachusetts, so I rooted for the Celtics during those epic battles. And when there were no games to watch, my imagination played out its own fan fiction of the rivalry: Larry Bird drawing a double team and finding me under the hoop for an easy two; banging bodies with A. C. Green and Kareem Abdul Jabbar; Kevin McHale checking into the game to replace me, the young buck, with the familiar high five of true teammates as we pass. I could smell the leather of the game ball on my hands.

These dreams were so vivid. That they might also be insane— the idea that I couldn't become one of the best 300 players in the world—never occurred to me. Improbable? Yes. But not impossible.

The most imposing obstacle was my severely limited set of technical skills and a lack of real knowledge of the strategic side of the game. But, given time, I knew I could acquire those. I knew my size enhanced my chance for success. And, importantly, I knew that I had a "cabinet" of allies who would support my ambition and help in my quest.

Sharing your goals with others in a measured, intentional way can help you find and connect with potential allies. This is not about catastrophizing about your areas of development or those moments where your resolve falters, but rather sharing openly that you don't think that what you're attempting will be—to use basketball parlance—a "layup" (that's a relatively easy shot, even for a beginner!) and as such you're going to need some help from time to time.

When I committed those words to the yearbook, I was codifying my intent in a clear and permanent way. But I was also inviting others to join me. If we're not willing to put ourselves out there and be bold—and we're not able to show that we don't have all the answers—then the kind of people we attract might not be the help we hope for. When people join a quest in the pursuit of a challenging goal, they need to see where they can add value and be needed. They need to know that there will be moments where their vision might improve your blind spots; if you appear invulnerable, it makes it both harder to contribute and less rewarding to do so. The kind of person who follows someone who purports to be invulnerable might be one who knows they have little to offer, and who, knowing that they will be asked for nothing, just comes along for the ride.

In the context of leadership, people don't *follow* someone they see as invulnerable, no matter how difficult the challenge. They are simply walking behind, along the easily traversed path cleared by the leader. They aren't on a quest with you, engaged in your travails and the challenges that are presented, poised at any moment to offer an essential nugget of insight or wisdom that will propel the group forward; no, they are human remoras—doing no harm, except adding a little drag, there for the ride and the scraps of "free food" that come from the leader's kills.

Creating a true "cabinet" means everyone has a role—everyone is essential for the successful completion of the quest, even when some roles are larger and some less so. Without any one person the chances of success are lessened. Essentially, with a true cabinet, part of the role of the cabinet is a continuously supportive and challenging investment in the leader—an investment that is absent when those accompanying the leader are simply swimming in their wake.

My greatest ally, naturally, was my mother, who recognized that a goal as bold as mine required a detailed plan of attack. Together, we designed that plan and defined explicitly what it would demand of me at each step of the way. Always, it demanded time in the gym. Always, it demanded avoiding the foods I most craved. But, in the beginning, it also demanded writing letters. Lots and lots of letters.

Early into our plan, my mum and I took the bus to the US Embassy in London to update my American passport (I am a dual national) and collect information related to studying in the States. At the Fulbright Commission office, we found a book that contained the addresses of every high school in America. It was an incredible resource in a pre-Internet world, and, as my mother would note on the bus ride home, it was "the most expensive book we've ever bought."

Working backward from the destination, to get to the NBA, I knew I needed to be drafted from a Division I NCAA school. And I knew we couldn't afford tuition at one of those schools without the assistance of a full scholarship. But neither my grades nor my athletic accomplishments warranted such a scholarship. So we reasoned that, even though I was finishing up my secondary school in the UK, I needed one year in an American high school to develop my game and gain exposure to college recruiters. This is where the book came in handy. It was 1988, long before the convenience of email, so I gathered a stack of paper and a stack of envelopes, and I started writing:

"Dear Coach. My name is John Amaechi. I am 17 years old, 6' 9", British, and Black. I am looking for a place to begin pursuing my dream of playing basketball in the NBA."

Beyond this, I provided a few details around my academic scores and the teams I'd played on. But, essentially, the words above comprised the extent of my appeal, which I wrote over and over again, hundreds of times until hundreds became thousands. My mother provided the book, the paper, the envelopes, and the necessary postage. But the labor was left to me, a one-man assembly line. Write, fold, stuff, lick, press; write, fold, stuff, lick, press.

This proceeded for months, as I sent the letters from sea to shining sea. The distinction between the states was lost on me; to my understanding, America was one monolithic landmass where the sun always shines. So I would literally flip that high-school directory to any random page and start selecting schools based on nothing more than the sound of their names.

There were a few exceptions—schools that I targeted because of elite basketball programs I'd read about in various articles—the Maryland rivals, DeMatha and Dunbar High, and St. Anthony's in New Jersey. For these coaches, without Mum's knowledge, I included a self-addressed return envelope, pre-stamped for their convenience, albeit with British postage stamps that I didn't realize would be useless to them.

I sent these in batches, and it was easy to be methodical and motivated early on. There was a romance to the mundanity of write, fold, stuff, lick, press ... I was a purposeful young Padawan, pacing through the grunt work that would launch a hero's journey. Filmmakers would capture it in montage—the early years sequence, cutting from me sweating in the gym to me toiling over my carefully organized stack of letters, cranking through them like a machine. "Putting in the work." Write, fold, stuff, lick, press ... Glory lay ahead.

The romance faded as the weeks passed without a single response. I was writing the same words, but they felt less like the words of a young hero and more like those of a naked fool. I imagined the coach having a laugh and then fixing the letter to a bulletin board for the team to see, for the school to see, for the entire community to gather round and get a laugh of their own. *Get a load o' this sad and desperate kid who thinks he can play basketball in America!* I was hanging exposed from the bulletin boards of 3,000 American high schools. Three thousand!

That's how many letters I wound up sending, expecting a flood of responses that never came. Eventually, though, three trickled in. The first was a polite rejection along the lines of "Thanks for reaching out. Aren't you ambitious? Best of luck but definitely no."

The second took a decidedly different tone, but also no. The coach made clear—and these few words, I do remember verbatim—that, as the "winningest high school in our state," they did not need any help from "foreign talent." Alrighty then, coach. A simple no would have sufficed or even no reply at all, but point taken. Thank you.

The third was the one that I needed. It came from a coach at St. John's Jesuit High School in Toledo, Ohio, Ed Heintschel. He had ties to coaches in Britain, and after receiving my letter, he dug around and learned enough to know that I wasn't full of it and might be worth a chance. I had no idea at the time, but in Coach Heintschel I'd found a lifelong ally. He brought me to the States, committed to preparing me for elite-level competition, and remains a friend to this day.

As a side note, when Coach Heintschel retired, I flew to Toledo from London for just 12 hours to see the dedication of my high-school gym in his honor. Quality time is how I show I care—and I wanted to show him that I realize I couldn't have been the person I am or the player I was without him.

I recount the yearbook and the stacks of letters because I'm positive that I benefited from repeatedly, openly and boldly stating my mission in clear terms. It led me to people and opportunities, and it strengthened my resolve. Each time I declined to join friends after school, telling them I had to go to the gym because that's what it takes to get to the NBA, I was pledging allegiance to my cause. If they rolled their eyes, that was OK. In fact, all the better because it motivated me. I was fortunate that, while many people did laugh and roll their eyes, I did find a curious group of friends—some of whom are my closest even to this day—who never rolled eyes, but supported and challenged me to deliver on my promises.

Being bold and vulnerable can be as simple as a public statement of intent. It is saying: *This is what I plan to do. I may not know exactly how I'm going to do it yet. But it is important that this thing be done, and thus, I will do what it takes.* It is laying intentions bare before even knowing the framework for how they'll be realized. From research we can see that, by sharing goals specifically and objectively with as many people as possible, we are more likely to hold ourself and be held accountable to them. Setting goals and subsequently monitoring them was related to future goal attainment. When the goal was declared publicly, the possibility of attaining future goals increased.[1]

It should go without saying, of course, that announcing a goal is not reaching a goal. "Speaking it into existence" isn't an actual thing (despite what some pundits tell you). But the initial rush of setting out on a new journey can be powerful and satisfying in its own right. So while boldness and vulnerability don't require a fully developed framework around your intentions, they do require thoughtfulness and accountability. An actionable statement of intent cannot simply be the casual resolution you share during a New Year's toast or a quick hit on social media:

"Just bought a juicer and I'm sheddin' 20 pounds by summer! #slamminbeachbod"

Like. Happy face emoji. Inspirational gif from *The Biggest Loser*. More likes. "You got this!" Fist bump emoji. Still more likes.

The immediate feedback feels amazing—or at least better than the feeling of anything remotely associated with losing 20 pounds.

And the danger is that the support and praise seduce you into feeling as though you've already accomplished something. And maybe you take your foot off the gas. The "likes" cloud your vision, causing you to underestimate the complexity of the task at hand.

We can mitigate this danger by creating a bold and personally challenging goal and explicitly calling for assistance and accountability—by making ourselves vulnerable. So share the initial ideas you have to achieve this goal, beyond buying the juicer. Ask how others have been successful. Encourage them to check on your progress and to hold you accountable when you're together. Open yourself to people who have already achieved something of the same order of magnitude as you hope to achieve, even if it's in a different context or sector. Seek out people who are farther along in their journey than you, and be bold in the face of whatever feedback results from that.

Throw out your cool card—that card you keep in your hip pocket to prevent you from feeling or appearing foolish, flawed, irreverent, or even unabashedly joyful. It's an anchor on your ambition, and you need to get rid of it. Which is not to say that you must be in a mode of absolute disclosure at all times.

So don't flay yourself until you're naked and raw with emotion. But do be appropriate for the moment. Do be human. There's an ill-conceived ideal of the stoic leader, robotically guiding the ship from behind an impenetrable veil. If they experience uncertainty or concern or happiness, you'd never know. They are superhuman. The problem is, the rest of us are not. If you seem superhuman, very few people can relate to you in any real way, which makes them reluctant followers. When a personal quest or an organizational strategy enters a period of intense disruption, it is perfectly normal and predictable for that to generate some level of nervousness and apprehension. Strong leaders acknowledge when they feel this themselves. If you can't reveal at least a hint of your actual state, it makes the people around you nervous about their own nervousness, as if there's something wrong with them for feeling as they do.

Practicing vulnerability allows for emotional pre-recognition, a necessary skill for leaders. This is the idea that we approach every situation by anticipating how it might affect the emotions of those around us. From there, we can tap into our own feelings and our own understanding of the situation to develop a strategy that puts everyone at ease. Or at least lets them feel normal for feeling out of sorts. During difficult times or even crises, it is saying:

> "Yes, the anxiety you're feeling is absolutely appropriate and shared. Here are some insights into myself, some experiences and some basic tools that I draw from to help me manage my emotions. Because you must know that, while you may have worries, I do, too. But I've considered them and have planned around them, and here is how we're going to conquer them together and move forward."

Expressing your own vulnerability allows you to connect with people in a way that can facilitate their development or improve their outlook. Women who are potential future leaders (in a world with a distinct bias against women leaders) benefit from hearing the hard lessons learned by women who've blazed that trail: their challenges and worries are normalized, and they gain practical insights into how they might overcome imposter syndrome or the inscrutable workplace standard of femininity. These issues can be effectively addressed by the sharing of experience.

It was only a chapter ago, but it bears reminding that these promises are not merely "nice to have". Boldness and vulnerability are necessary for evolution, for harnessing change. When I started consulting, I assumed the greatest challenge would be motivating good organizations to become great. This seemed logical, and as it turns out, it is indeed quite difficult to inspire change when the existing state is "good." However, it also turns out to be true that it's equally difficult to inspire change when the existing state is bad. Once a condition has been in place for more than, say, six months, it earns a sort of tenure. Whether the condition is good, bad, terrible, or brilliant doesn't much matter. The volatility of change and any transitional work that it may demand are generally viewed as less palatable than even the dreariest status quo.

People of a certain age grew up believing in the sanctity and endurance of institutions—governments, corporations, places of worship, universities. In the UK, people viewed these things as they viewed Stonehenge: a historical monument that would stand forever, revered by the masses. Without adaptation to not only tolerate change but actively pursue it, institutions risk becoming what Stonehenge is today—a wondrous, yet sad and decrepit, stone circle, scrutinized by niche groups of experts who are still trying to decide what it ever was in the first place. It's virtually ignored by travelers who speed past it day after day on the highway only yards away, and now it looks as though they'll be tunneling an underpass beneath it, so soon no one will see it at all.

It is not the indomitable who will lead the way through crises and disruption. This was stated elegantly in 1963 by a Louisiana State University business professor named Leon C. Megginson. Commenting on Charles Darwin's *On the Origin of Species*, Megginson wrote, "It is not the most intellectual of the species that survives; it is not the strongest that survives; but the species that survives is the one that is able to adapt to, and to adjust best to, the changing environment in which it finds itself."

This is literally why we're here. Millions of years ago, a meteor the size of Everest, moving so fast that it would still have been invisible 30 minutes before it hit the planet, wiped out 80 percent of life on Earth. And when the dust settled, the almighty dinosaurs (with the exception of the ancestors of birds) were nowhere to be seen. What emerged from the rubble were tiny mammals who were able to take advantage of the sudden obliteration of the primary predators that once ruled. Over time, these creatures would persist and evolve, thriving in their changed environment.

The dinosaurs of course had no foreknowledge of their demise, as is often the case. The days leading to collapse and ruin of a dynasty can be indistinguishable from the long stretches of success and dominance that precede. During those heady, last days, enemies have been identified and slain or cowed. Boundaries have long been established, and norms are accepted even by those who don't like them. Dissidents are barely a distraction—flies to be swatted away or nudged into line. Prosperity and order rule the day, and the empire is secure. Until it is not.

For now, at least, the reckoning that faces us is less immediate and thorough in its devastation than a meteor striking the Earth. But not by much! Historically speaking, it was not long ago that Megginson wrote about "the changing environment" to which we all must adapt. But in 1963 it would have been tough for Megginson or anyone to imagine the depths of tumult or the complexity and variety of societal shifts that define our present state.

Now is not the time to coast on cruise control. Nor is it the time to rely on history and tradition and assume that will be enough. At its best, tradition grounds us in the past; it provides a foundation for a culture that promotes shared values and purpose. At its worst, tradition is an anchor—a barrier to boldness and a security blanket that conceals our vulnerabilities. It is immutable, suspicious of change, and a prisoner to the past. Used as a crutch, tradition favors tenure and homogeneity, protecting members with similar backgrounds and experiences. To work for the present and the future, tradition must be subject to fulsome scrutiny and open to amendment in the service of the developing interests of all parties, not only leadership.

The Promises of Giants is a promise to race toward a tomorrow that will not look like today. And this promise cannot be kept without being bold in our ambition and acknowledging our vulnerabilities to ourselves and those with whom we quest.

It will feel risky and at times even frightening, but the potential rewards are immense and there for the taking. If we can approach life with the courage and enthusiasm of that eager child who is unashamed of their dreams, we lift the ceiling on creativity, innovation, accountability, compassion, and resiliency. If we cannot—if we are seduced by the status quo or fearful of what could result from truly extending ourselves—we are likely to find ourselves in a similar spot as Stonehenge. Slowly aging along the side of the road, questioning our relevance as the world passes us by.

Activity: What is *Your* Ambition?

Ambition is always relative. Some of you may be comfortably ensconced in business; others may be thinking about a transition in role or stage of life; still others may be new to planning for the future. Whichever of these groups you belong to, you will have a different challenge you'd like to tackle.

The question is, then: what is your grand challenge; what is your next bold goal? You've begun to understand yourself better using the "Soul in the Dark" exercise in Chapter 1, so now might be a good time to use those early findings to decide what kind of goals or ambitions are going to be meaningful and give you a sense of purpose and achievement, both during the journey and at your destination.

You don't have to make this a five-year plan, but something that will require you to both really stretch yourself and be bold and to embrace a bit of jeopardy and be vulnerable.

Think about the goals and ambitions you've daydreamed or dreamed about—what can they tell you about a possible goal?

Think about the stories you've shared with friends and partners about the future—are there any themes that develop that might suggest a bold goal?

CHAPTER 4

I Promise to Act with Vigilance Against My Biases

It would be ridiculous if I didn't mention at the start that we have been sensitized to inequity over recent years, in a way that some have never previously understood and about which others are still coming to grips. To take just the most publicized of examples, the murder of George Floyd in Minneapolis in 2020 created a tidal wave of emotions and resonant anti-racism demonstrations and outpourings of emotion in more than 60 countries around the world.

While my team and I are doing a lot of work in businesses and third-sector organizations trying to create substantive and strategic approaches to equity for all, including for racial minorities, this book is not a primer on that work. This chapter is a broader statement about all of us, with all our biases, and the need for us to be vigilant to them if we want to create authentic connections with people based on the quality of their character, not on their gender, color of skin, or any other identity category. If we want to succeed in this world—to solve the big, new challenges and create the solutions that will be essential not only for our own success but for our collective survival—then we will need to live, work, and collaborate with people vastly different from ourselves. As organizations and individuals we will need effective ways to combat bias, and we will need to eschew those methods that continue to fail us and those individuals who refuse to develop the skills and capabilities to engage with people different from themselves.

Imagine for a moment that you've badly injured your foot. Perhaps you slammed it in the car door or dropped something heavy on it. Whatever the case, you suspect it is likely broken because it's swollen and bruised and the pain is excruciating. So you drag your mangled foot to the doctor's office and they help you into the examination room, where patiently you wait.

Imagine this all, please. Visualize it clearly in your mind's eye. See yourself sitting on the metal table, leafing through a tabloid that is of no interest of you, just to distract your mind from the pain. The disposable paper under your bottom crinkles and crackles each time you shift your weight. Finally, the doctor strides confidently through the door, clipboard in hand, ready to diagnose, treat, and put you on the road to recovery. Picture this entrance, envision this doctor. Look into the eyes of this doctor. Who do you see?

If you see a woman, I would put down odds that you're either a woman yourself or you're a graduate of "anti-bias" training, who is already wise to theoretical scenarios and riddles designed to illuminate your preconceptions. This is not one of those. I don't buy into any of this unconscious bias nonsense and my company will not sell it to you. "Unconscious" is a thing, yes, and "bias" is a thing, yes. Just like "marzipan" is a thing and "bicycle" is a thing. But "unconscious bias" is not a thing, any more than a "marzipan bicycle" is a thing. And it is frankly outrageous that organizations focus so heavily on this non-thing at the expense of addressing actual actions and behaviors. Unconscious bias training is absolute bunkum and has become a harmful distraction in the workplace. But perhaps I'm ahead of myself.

Let's return to your foot. We left you in agony on the examination table, so we should probably patch you up. Imagine the doctor again, and feel free to switch doctors this time if it makes you feel better about yourself or the sins of your ancestors. You can pick one right out of minority central casting if you wish—maybe a woman doctor or a Black man doctor or a Black woman doctor in a wheelchair even ... that would be radical. But once you have the image in your mind, imagine the doctor examining your wounded foot with all the seriousness you would hope for and expect. Delicately applying pressure to different areas. Asking, "Does it hurt here?

How about here?" Jotting down notes. Nodding earnestly. A quick X-ray is taken, and the foot is still throbbing, but there's relief in knowing you're in good hands. And eventually the doctor, having collected all of the information, confirms what you suspected all along. "You've broken the foot, I'm afraid. You've broken it real good. But if you'll give me a moment, I'll be right back and we'll fix you up like new."

The doctor exits and before long returns with what appears to be a black shoebox. You're a tad confused as it's set down beside you because, indeed, you now see clearly that there is a red Nike logo splashed across the front. What is going on? The doctor waits a beat to elevate the drama before removing the lid and unfolding the tissue paper for the big reveal.

"The Air Jordan 1, you remember these? Michael Jordan's first signature shoe. Classic red-and-black colorway. Launched in 1985, his rookie season. Retail value of only $65 back then, hard to find nowadays. An iconic sneaker. What do you think?"

Uhh. "They're fine," you say. "But ..."

"This design revolutionized the entire footwear industry—not just basketball sneakers. Our feet never looked the same after these came along. For that matter, advertising and branding were never the same! Go ahead, please! Try them on."

So you try them on. Doctor's orders, after all. You jam your swollen foot into one and slip your healthy foot into the other. And maybe you're a fan of the look or maybe you think they're better suited for a clown. But your primary reaction is confusion.

"How do they feel?" the doctor asks. "Do they fit? I have the black as well if the red and black is too much."

"No, no, it's not that," you reply. "The color is fine. They fit OK."

"Well, they look wonderful on you," the doctor replies, beaming with admiration. "You need to wear these every day for the next three months and that broken foot will be all set."

Far be it from you to question the authority of a doctor, but at this point you have to ask: "So I'm to wear these basketball shoes from the mid-1980s, and that alone will heal my broken foot?"

"You're gonna feel like a million bucks," the doctor confirms while taking some final notes. "They really look fantastic on you."

"Right, but if I may, how does this work? I'm still in quite a bit of pain here, and I don't see how these sneakers alone are going to help the bone repair itself. Do you need to do something else before I start wearing them?"

"No no, just the sneakers and you are golden. You'll be up and running in no time."

"How can that be, though? How does it work?"

The doctor is unflappable. "I can't really tell you that. What I can tell you is we've prescribed these Air Jordans to 90 percent of the patients who come to us with broken feet. So you need not worry."

"Right, but did they get better?" you ask. "Did the sneakers heal all of those broken feet? Were there results?"

The doctor has no answer. Just gives a shrug of the shoulders, hands over your discharge papers, and wishes you the best of luck before leaving the examination room.

Such is unconscious bias training in a nutshell. The proverbial lipstick on a pig. It is neither a strategic nor systemic approach to confronting actual problems of bias and exclusion. But it provides cover; it gives the appearance of caring. It is an obvious effort that can be deployed quickly and at scale, and that—not effectiveness—is its primary appeal.

In a context where *recognizing* bias is the problem, training has value. But, in most workplaces, the problem is not recognition of bias, "unconscious" or otherwise; it is the behaviors that *result* from those biases. If the misbehavior that stems from bias is not properly addressed (and it usually is not), then unconscious bias training is as counterproductive as treating a broken foot with a new pair of sneakers.

There is an amazing researcher named Susan Michie, professor of health psychology at University College London and director of the college's Centre for Behaviour Change. She is the mother of behavior change, and her work has helped me realize that behavior change—of our personal behaviors and those promulgated and, indeed, tolerated by our institutions—is key. My organization's spin on Dr. Michie's work focuses on her four elements of behavior change:

1. **Knowledge**—the "awareness" that everyone talks about in current training—necessary, but not sufficient

2. **Capabilities**—the skills and tools that enable people to interact and intervene effectively, to remain vigilant in personal interactions and help others do the same

3. **Opportunity**—creating access for and to the right moments to utilize capabilities

4. **Motivation**—building an enduring motivation to act well and consistently.

I have never been wounded by a racist or homophobic thought. It's unlikely you have been either ... You've been wounded by what people *do* to and around you, even if that action is to not engage or not care.

Instinctively picturing a theoretical doctor as a man is not in and of itself a grave sin, nor is it unusual. My mother was a doctor and spent her entire career being referred to as "the lady doctor." I am the director of a hospital trust with nine hospitals and 29,000 staff and clinicians, where many of our most talented surgeons are women. And yet in the course of a conversation, if someone generically alludes to a "doctor," I too sometimes catch myself envisioning a man. But what do I *do* with that preconceived notion? And just as importantly, what do I *not* do?

I challenge my own preconceptions *before* they leave my brain as speech or action.

Everyone harbors bias. It is not something to be proud of, but it's also not something to self-flagellate over to excess. You don't need to feel guilty for being white or guilty for being male or straight. Doing so benefits no one.

But if you are in those categories, it is critical that you appreciate and understand your inherent privilege and how it affects your worldview. The concept of privilege is often misunderstood and overly personalized. It is not about being rich or blessed with a life free of discomfort. It's about the distinct advantage secured only by being born into a certain identity. They often come in the form of an absence of a particular impediment, which means we often don't realize we have these privileges when they're present because their impact only crystalizes with their absence.

Research makes it abundantly clear, for example, that a poor white man has a better chance of improving his lot in life than does an equally poor white woman. And if he does—if he "earns" and attains a better future—we can celebrate that effort without dismissing the fact that better futures are often "earned" but not attained by those from less privileged categories.

It might be helpful for you to watch a video I did for the BBC, talking about privilege, as it goes into more detail on how understanding privilege is a benefit to all: www.bbc.co.uk/bitesize/articles/zrvkbqt

I am sympathetic to the well-meaning, white, middle-class men who grapple with discussions of privilege. It is understandably a complex reality for them to embrace, fraught with potentially painful personal revelations and unnecessary guilt. But it is imperative that everyone does this work. If you don't appreciate your privilege, you do actual damage just by your dismissal of its existence.

Similarly, it is imperative that we appreciate the existence of our biases and do everything possible to prevent them from negatively influencing our actions and behaviors. For the last few years, I've led our clients through an experiment to explore what they think about certain identities, as well as, perhaps, what they deny thinking. Because what we label as "unconscious" is often just stuff we prefer to believe never crosses our mind. They are "covert" or "implicit" rather than "overt" bias, and that distinction is really more accurate than "conscious" versus "unconscious."

In the experiment, audience members have 90 seconds to jot down the words that they associate with a particular identity, be it Black, gay, woman, trans, and so on. And then they are given 90 seconds to jot down what they believe other people associate with those identities. So, for example, we have asked roughly 10,000 respondents over three continents to share their associations with different identities.

- For "the LGBT+ community" people's top words were:
  ◦ Gay, Equality, Lesbian, Rainbow, Pride, Love.

- When asked what they believed other people thought, they said:
  ◦ Different, Gay, Strange, Wrong, Weird, Hate.

- For "women," people's top words were:
  ◦ Strong, Weak, Mother, Caring, Beautiful, Determined.

- When asked what others thought of "women," the responses got distinctly worse:
  ◦ Emotional, Weak, Mother, Sexy, Annoying, Cleaning.

- For Black people, the most common answers are complimentary, but stereotypical:
  ◦ Strong, Athletic, Beautiful, Proud, Sports, Music.

- However, when asked how *others* perceive Black people, the answers notably diverge:
  ◦ Criminal, Athletic, Poor, Lazy, Uneducated, Scary.

This juxtaposition of responses between what we say *we* associate with identities and what we know *other people* associate with those same identities is consistent from identity to identity.

There is a clear split, with a group of more flattering—if unhelpfully stereotypical—associations made by individual respondents and a group of far more negative associations made on behalf of other people.

The consistent results here beg the question that, if thousands of people all claim to possess such positive associations but unanimously believe that others have negative associations, then who are those "others"? Respondents claim not to personally harbor these negative associations, and yet they find it remarkably easy to create a list of them in just 90 seconds. How can this be? It's almost impossible to have that kind of access to those perceptions if they're not already living in some form in your head.

It's worth noting that we've asked these questions in people's offices across the world and the individual pictures across countries are near identical, with some differences for the gender picture in China. There is a global consistency of associations with identities and a global consistency in a reticence to acknowledge our own prejudice that is enabling its perpetuation.

Biases reside in all of us, and we must do everything possible to prevent them from negatively influencing our actions and behaviors. These biases will be with us each time we meet a new coworker and will shape the way we receive information from panel discussions and presentations. They will flash before us as we're deciding where to sit on the train, as we're writing a job description or considering who is best suited for a project. This is why we must promise to act with vigilance against bias. It is not going away, and its influence on behavior can be toxic.

I've attended industry functions where I felt welcomed within the confines of the convention center or hotel ballroom. Outside, though—where the lanyards come off—the reception is often more complicated. Maybe it's after hours and I'm returning from a late-night beverage or maybe I'm wandering the streets in sweatpants, trying to find my first coffee of the day. In those situations, the same people who might have embraced me in the industry context will be perceptibly more guarded. My appearance triggers their fight-or-flight response and initiates a mental assessment of the threat level I pose. It happens with lightning speed, but I've seen it enough to spot it with ease.

"Hmmm, Black guy. Really massive Black guy. Massive Black guys frighten me and are dangerous. I'm going to be really tense until I figure out what to do with this fear caused by this potentially dangerous Black guy."

If I were to concede that "unconscious bias" is a thing, then I suppose the reaction described here would serve as one such example. These people are not necessarily racists, right? Their response is a natural outcome from decades of false narratives promoted by society and the media. Does that matter though, really? In those moments, the source and the existence of bias is a secondary concern. The primary concern is what people *do*. What is the conscious action that is taken after you identify your fear as unfounded, the product of nonsense? Do you cross the street to avoid the massive Black guy, "just to be safe"? Do you take a deliberate action that plays into or further enforces the mythology engrained in your psyche?

Every day we invigilate "semi-reflexive" thoughts, putting hooks on those that should not rise to the surface. If a colleague shares a terribly stupid idea, you're probably able to react in a way that does not make the colleague feel stupid. If you're at a restaurant and your server is unbearably attractive, you can hopefully get through dessert without acting upon each act of lust that runs through your head. If a neighbor's toddler proudly shows you their drawing of a dog and it's unrecognizable as anything at all, much less a dog, you don't tell them it's crap, right? In these and literally thousands of other ways, we attenuate our first responses on a daily basis.

We do not say or act on everything we think, in part because if we did, it would be the Wild West. We take what our brain "tells" us to do, and in a split second we consider that response against the fallibility and fragility of humans, the imperfection and variance of perceptions, accepted standards of decency, and our own self-interests. We rely on those hooks to invigilate our primal thoughts and responses.

The unconscious bias narrative inextricably links thoughts to their resultant actions. It focuses on identifying and monitoring bias in our thinking because thoughts tainted by bias are inherently destined to manifest as actions. This disregards the fact that, in every other aspect of our lives, we are able to disentangle thoughts from actions. Worse, it gives latitude to bad behavior. If the relationship between thoughts and actions is fixed and if biased thoughts are "unconscious"—implanted by forces beyond our control—then, by extension, the actions that were preordained to emerge from those thoughts are also beyond our control.

Corporate diversity and inclusion efforts would be better off focusing on behavior and rhetoric, as opposed to individual biased thoughts. This may seem a subtle difference. But we are not the thought police. In the workplace, we cannot control whether our colleagues harbor racist, sexist, or otherwise unsavory thoughts— conscious or unconscious, overt or covert. It is not our job to evolve their thinking. It is our job to ensure that nobody is impacted by that type of thinking manifest in behavior. Our attention should be focused on what people say and what they do, on rhetoric and behavior. Words and actions can be observed, measured, challenged, sanctioned, and rewarded. Words and actions are where actual damage is done.

This is not to trivialize principles and beliefs and values and the way that we think. But the truth is, all of that is meaningless if it's not supported by actions. It is the individual everyday actions and behaviors of colleagues, managers, and leaders that drive organizational culture. Actions are what count—the things that we *choose* to do. They can have radical effects on people. They can inspire or deflate. They can turn allies against each other, and they can unite strangers behind a shared vision.

Actions motivated my mother to change my name when I was 11. I can assure you that she did not take that step because of what people might think or feel. Her concern was what they might *do*. She understood that, sight unseen, John Amaechi would get a fairer shake in life than Uzoma Ekwugha Amaechi. That was my given name. It's Nigerian—beautiful and powerful and 100 percent more bad-ass than "John" (with no disrespect intended toward my fellow Johns). John Amaechi is perceived as harmless and likely a white Italian. Uzoma Ewkugha Amaechi, on the other hand, is perceived as fresh off the boat and likely still wearing tribal gear. My mother knew the advantages that "John" would have over "Uzoma" in academia and the job market, so the change was made.

Again, my mother didn't make that decision because a hiring manager might one day look at my CV and have a good laugh. "What a funny little name this is! Must be a foreigner of some kind!" That reaction would not be ideal, agreed. But if it was the extent of the damage—an initial, contained, and fleeting response tainted by "unconscious bias"—it wouldn't really be worth changing a name. My mother was guarding against the resultant *conscious* actions. Does the hiring manager have a laugh and then drop my CV in the trash because "Uzoma" sounds like a "bad fit"? If I'm somehow hired, will I be marginalized by colleagues who crinkle their face when they say "Uzoma," as if swallowing sour milk? Who always follow the name by saying, "Or however it's pronounced"? Will I be overlooked for opportunities by senior leaders who know little about me beyond a weird name that tells them I'm barely literate?

These were not baseless worries; my mother was not paranoid. We know that applicants with names perceived to be white get 50 percent more callbacks—even when the resumes are identical.[1]

Non-white applicants have to make between 70–90 percent more applications to get a callback,[2] and indeed, as my mum feared, yet more research has illustrated that for Black people "whitened" resumés that change names and make no reference to ethnicity get 2.5 times more callbacks than identical resumes that don't.[3]

There were, and are, people with tremendous power and influence who just aren't vigilant about their biases. And that lack of vigilance poisons opportunity for individuals and entire organizations. But, rather than deal with our words and deeds, we focus on changing our mind, and this has the effect of allowing an absurdly long timeline for tangible change in people's experience of inequity.

Embracing "unconscious bias" gives a free pass to "work on your-self" over an indeterminate period of time and a sense of auto-matic immunity from scorn from those who are "working it out in their head" and yet still behaving poorly.

Unconscious bias should be more accurately described as "entrenched assumption," to stop people thinking they're dealing with an inaccessible slice of their psyche that they could not have been aware of and thus are not responsible for. It's easier to believe our own bias is the product of some hidden dumping ground for prej-udices passed down by our parents, our hometown, and our child-hood experiences. And the best we can do is accept the existence of these biases and apologize if they surface in the form of bad behavior.

This perspective is a perfect storm of "It's not my fault," "I was powerless to prevent it," and "People should be grateful that I'm acknowledging it." It is not a recipe for action, and it is certainly not enough. Someone else may have left a pile of junk in your attic, but you're responsible for it now and it's your job to clean it up. Unconscious bias training fails to demand that of people, and to fulfill this promise, we must recognize that to make a difference in this world, to create the coalitions that spawn innovation and sustain success, it's not enough to change our mind—we have to change our behavior.

Organizations will proudly cite the number of people who have completed unconscious bias training as evidence of the training's effectiveness. Again, this is, to be kind, odd. It is all well and good if 97 percent of staff participates in the training. But does the training have any meaningful impact on the organization's recruitment, retention, succession, or engagement numbers? Does anything change for the better? Do the Air Jordans fix the broken foot? Or are 97 percent of staff now limping around in slightly more supportive shoes? Isn't the organization just checking a box and giving a mere nod to the junk in its attic?

There is mounting research that questions whether uncon-scious bias training has had any meaningful effect on workplaces. This should not be surprising, given the target audience. Google, as one example, has reportedly invested at least $200 million in unconscious bias training. But if Google and similar industry giants attract the best of the best—the sharpest minds and the most creative thinkers—then shouldn't it stand to reason that their workforce is sophisticated enough to be cognizant of their biases? How dumb and shallow do we believe our people to be if we think they've lived their entire lives haunted by ghosts that are only now being revealed through this magical training?

Of course, even in forward-thinking organizations, an unenlightened few will slip through the cracks—people who live in a weird bubble and are only just realizing that Black people can be doctors or women can be executives. But, for the most part, people do know better. Unconscious bias training advocates claim it brings greater awareness, but awareness itself doesn't fix problems and this supposed lack of awareness is a myth to begin with. The vast majority of people well understand the diversity, inequities, and prejudices of society, as evidenced by how quickly respondents are able to list negative stereotypes in the experiment discussed earlier.

It is unlikely you will find anyone in your workplace who is unaware of the reality of bias. You're more likely to find people who understand its effect on the organization but lack the motivation to fight it. Some will just be passive and lazy. Resigned to a belief that matters of inclusion and diversity are beyond their control. And as long as they view themselves as both unaffected by the problem and innocent of contributing to it, they're happy to cruise along with the status quo.

Others will more actively protect that status quo because their success depends upon it. Every large organization has some population of tenured individuals who benefit from the imbalanced playing field. For them, inclusion and outsiders are threats, and the bias in their language and behavior acts as a weapon against that threat. They are mediocre performers, but they are by no means dumb. In fact, they are quite clever at manifesting their biases in effective ways that act as a hand brake on change while toeing the line of what's acceptable. They are adept at circumventing policies and undercutting initiatives in ways that are not obvious. Their actions are subtle, and their language is nuanced and often excused as mere humor or banter. They are masters of skirting sanction while helping to preserve the status quo of power and privilege. And all of their actions are taken consciously, with full knowledge of the impact their behavior will have on those who aren't like them.

The unconscious bias narrative avoids an honest assessment of exclusion and inequality or a strategy for how to deal with them. It provides cover for bad actors—a level of plausible deniability—and, for organizational leaders, it provides an opportunity to look and feel like agents of change without exerting the effort that change requires. That is its primary appeal: the training can be executed broadly at a relatively low cost, with minimal ruffling of feathers. It may not diversify recruiting classes or improve retention numbers, but it's easy to deploy. At a reasonable expense, the training can be administered to tens of thousands of employees over a few hours. And when annual reports are published, the percentage of workers who have completed training can be proudly shared with boards, investors, and watchdogs. Pats on the back all the way around!

Leaders and true agents of change cannot rely on this nonsense. The bar is much higher than simply acknowledging the existence of "personally unauthorized" bias. We must promise vigilance against it, every day and every hour. In our organizations, there must be tangible sanctions for inappropriate behavior, even if it forces us to confront or part ways with toxic but tenured and otherwise productive employees. Directly addressing, with swift and unflinching zeal, the actions that stem from bias will likely heighten tensions for a while. But actual progress cannot be achieved without actual discomfort—discomfort that exceeds being stuck in unconscious bias training with a burning desire to check your email and a lousy catered sandwich if you're lucky.

At the personal level, we must hold our own behavior to the highest standards and surround ourselves with a diverse and trusted cabinet of colleagues whom we empower to call us out when our vigilance falters. We must reject the passive victim mentality that is subtly endorsed by unconscious bias training and replace it with an active pairing of benign ignorance and enthusiastic inquisitiveness. This is the mindset from which I try to approach every introduction and interaction. If ever I meet you, I'll assume nothing and I'll want to know everything about you or at least all that you're willing to share.

I lived in Arizona for several years in my thirties, and my house had a hot tub in the back facing west across the desert landscape. And every evening that my schedule allowed, I would sit in that hot tub and watch the sunset over the saguaro cactus. It was magnificent—truly awe-inspiring. If you paid attention, you could see something new every night. Coyotes and the little warthogs called javelinas scurrying past. Hawks soaring above and hummingbirds flitting about. The brilliant transformation of colors across the sky until the sun finally disappeared, leaving the stage to the stars for their equally brilliant show.

When out-of-town guests would visit, I'd share this experience. We would sit on the patio for hours, gazing to the sky with wide-eyed wonder. That's how it would go the first night. On the second, most guests would be eager to see it all again. But more times than not, by an hour or so into that session, the novelty would start wearing off. And by the third night, it would often be competing for attention with reruns of *Law and Order*. The marvel of nature was no less spectacular, but by the third night it was a scene they thought they'd seen. They were wrong. Every night you could see or hear something new if you looked for it.

Those evenings forever shaped the way that I look at people—benign ignorance paired with enthusiastic inquisitiveness. Every new interaction is a sunset experienced anew. They are best appreciated if you arrive with no expectations, good or bad, based on previous sunsets. And if you pay close enough attention, they will invariably reveal something new. I am completely open to being amazed. I actively choose to believe that I know nothing about people, leaving the baggage of preconceived notions at the door.

Then I soak up whatever I can get. When someone comes into my circle, I make it clear that I want to learn as much from them as they'll allow. Tell me more, I'll eat it up. And I'll use that information—authentic disclosures, not a broad set of assumptions—to construct my impressions.

Applied with a growth mindset, benign ignorance and enthusiastic inquisitiveness create a foundation of empathy and a path toward understanding. They ensure that we don't botch relationships from the start, and they neutralize the influence of "schemas" that develop in our minds over the course of a lifetime. These schemas categorize what we've learned about ourselves and the world and prepare us to react accordingly. They provide preprogrammed responses to stimuli, and there was a time when they served us well. Prehistoric beings, for example, developed schemas that cautioned them to beware of animals bearing large teeth and sharp claws. They were part of a useful instinct for self-preservation.

But as the world has grown more complex, vast, and connected, schemas have become less reliable. They infer meaning from characteristics that could mean anything or nothing. I have dark skin and a white beard that is usually trimmed and well groomed. If I let it grow just the right amount, I suddenly start receiving "Allahu Akbar" greetings from my Muslim brethren on the street. I do not get that reaction when I shave. Based on a tiny and insignificant feature—barely an extra inch of scraggly facial hair—their schemas are signaling that I am one of them, when in fact I'm a gay atheist. So, in this case, we can safely say the schemas were not on point.

Schemas are shortcuts. If we've already assigned a certain set of responses to certain types of people, decision making becomes far less energy expensive. But, by doing so, what do we miss out on? Consider white, straight, alpha males somewhere between the ages of, say, 21 and 50. One could argue that, over the course of history, this population hasn't been the most benevolent in its treatment of others. At the least, we can say it's a group that has enjoyed and benefited from advantages that it's had a hand in maintaining. Nonetheless, if we write off that population altogether, we will miss out on incredible people! When I meet a white man of a certain age, I don't pretend that I have any insights into him despite the countless negative experiences I've had with white men of a certain age. Because I've also known remarkable individuals from this category who were absolutely formative in my life. And it's hard to countenance the idea that those individuals were just freakish outliers. It's more logical to believe that everyone is different and unique. And there will be effort required just to begin knowing them.

Today's workplaces are plagued with inequities that thwart any chance to improve productivity, engagement, or sustainable success. But those inequities will not be fixed with a session or two of unconscious bias training. It takes *action*. This is a promise to *act* with vigilance against bias, not just to concede its existence. That starts with the simple act of not being a jerk; that much should be straightforward. Treat people fairly, and be consistent in the application of your standards. Call out misbehavior when you see it, even when it's uncomfortable. It's not rocket science.

Beyond that, though, do the extra work to find the best in people. Approach every one of your colleagues as if they have boundless potential until they prove to you otherwise, consistently and without undue impediment. That last bit is so important, especially for minorities who may be negotiating environments with systemic constraints working against them. Despite the scales being tipped against their favor, their first mistake often becomes their last. It seals their fate and locks in their narrative. Their miscues are judged not as individual incidents but as confirmation that they're limited by their "otherness."

Stereotypes, biases, and schemas are all working together to promote assumptions, cloud your view, and influence your behavior. Do not let them. Act with vigilance against bias and embrace others with benign ignorance and enthusiastic inquisitiveness. I cannot say that you will never be let down. But more times than not, when granted the spotlight of your attention, like a desert sunset, people will put on a brilliant show.

To help you along this path, it can be useful to use a system called pragmatic self-assessment—outlined below—where you spend time reflecting on your own filters and biases—in this case, around interactions with people different than you—and replaying these interactions to learn if and why they went well or poorly. It's essential to gain feedback from peers and diverse colleagues and friends about your interactions with people. Have they seen any differences in your approach to different types of people?

You can commit to employing the vigilance we've been talking about throughout this chapter when it comes to each new human interaction—challenging each errant or dysfunctional, knee-jerk thought or response to a person and indeed those long-standing negative or lukewarm sentiments for a basis in fact, not bias. In doing so, you can create new connections with people who are different from you. There doesn't have to be a work program to create connections or even actual mentoring; you can create new relationships with people different than you without making those relationships *because* they're different. We can each choose to search for the qualities we like, admire, and respect in colleagues and friends and simply extend that search beyond those similar and familiar to us. It's likely you haven't spent much time thinking about these characteristics specifically, but if you're willing to categorize them, you'll be better able to spot them in people different than you. If they remain under wraps, then you'll likely go around assuming—as most of us do—that the qualities you like and admire (whatever they are) are more likely present in people who are similar and familiar to you.

You can use the following technique to start answering these questions. Replay scenarios that build friendships at work and socially, and consider what that person showed you to make you want to be a better colleague or friend. Ask your friends what they think you see in them and they in you.

When you have this burgeoning list, keep it top of mind and look for these qualities in everyone you meet. You'll be pleasantly surprised: you'll build a more diverse network, and you'll be armed with another tool to make you more vigilant against assumptions.

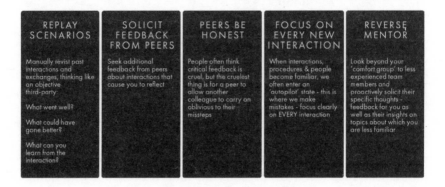

REPLAY SCENARIOS	SOLICIT FEEDBACK FROM PEERS	PEERS BE HONEST	FOCUS ON EVERY NEW INTERACTION	REVERSE MENTOR
Manually revisit past interactions and exchanges, thinking like an objective third-party. What went well? What could have gone better? What can you learn from the interaction?	Seek additional feedback from peers about interactions that cause you to reflect	People often think critical feedback is cruel, but the cruelest thing is for a peer to allow another colleague to carry on oblivious to their missteps	When interactions, procedures & people become familiar, we often enter an 'autopilot' state - this is where we make mistakes - focus clearly on EVERY interaction	Look beyond your 'comfort group' to less experienced team members and proactively solicit their specific thoughts - feedback for you as well as their insights on topics about which you are less familiar

Pragmatic self-assessment

Source: APS Intelligence, 2021

If you lead a team or an organization, it might be worth noting some of the ways that you can ensure that the training you do addresses the problem of the differential experience of people, rather than ticking another box. These elements include the following:

- **Focus on behavior change, not "awareness":** Organizations manage their people's behavior every single day, adding the component that ensures the dignity of all colleagues should not be controversial.

- **Follow an evidenced-based model:** such as those Dr. Michie and APS employ to ensure that all the elements of the behavior change model—Knowledge, Capabilities, Opportunities, and Motivation—are addressed.

- **Emotional scaffolding:** A particular instructional strategy that my team and I love—illustrated in the vignettes and stories interlaced in this book—is called emotional scaffolding.[4] Emotional scaffolding engages people's imagination—using metaphor, visual representations, or narratives of content—in an effort to foster a particular emotional response to technical and otherwise less interesting content.

- **Long-term practical learning:** The longer the training, the more effective it is (due to increased practice time, long-term exposure to new ideas, and contact with people who feel and think differently).

- **Mandatory participation:** People might like mandatory training less, but they are more likely to change their behaviors following it!

- **Content choice:** Giving people the chance to guide at least some parts of their own learning increases motivation to participate. Making some of the diversity and inclusion modules optional means the participants can choose the timing and combination of modules they need to complete mandatory training.

- **Perspective-taking:** Without oversimplifying too much, people are broadly split into those who regularly undertake perspective-taking—that is, they actively consider other people's situations and contexts and how they might think and feel if they experienced them—and those who almost never do (who number more than we might like to think). Content that facilitates perspective-taking validates the former group and is essential for the latter group as perhaps a first glimpse of "a mile in someone else's shoes."

- **Progress tracking:** It is crucial to systematically collect, analyze and evaluate a set of objective metrics for progress through any learning and development program. We can do this by defining the learning outcomes (what we want participants to get out of the sessions they attend) from the beginning of a program's creation and measuring individual and cohort progress towards those outcomes—as well as being willing to note any additional learnings or unintended consequences over time.

- **Concurrent amplification:** The change will more likely last if it's actively sustained through other diversity and inclusion activities, from reading clubs to discussion groups and team-based learning.

CHAPTER 5

I Promise to Reject Excuses and Embrace Discomfort

Excuses are easy to find. And when they're not immediately evident, they're easy to create. If, by chance, you've attempted to write a book, you know this as well as anyone! As I sit here today, it's lovely outside. I could be forgiven for wanting to escape my office and chase the sun rather than toil before the searing light of a monitor and the taunts of its blinking cursor. I've put in a full workweek already, and another lies ahead. The list of intriguing books I have yet to read keeps growing. There are friends I should catch up with. And, as noted earlier, I am an inherently lazy bastard, which means I'd be perfectly content to forgo all of those healthy excuses and instead grant myself a few hours on the couch watching an *Avengers* film I've already seen several times over.

Any of those options would be preferable to working on this book or, frankly, to working in general. Don't misunderstand, I love what I do. I love working with clients to help them get better. I love leading workshops that we've tailored to a specific audience, in a specific sector, with a very specific set of challenges. And, as an outsider, I love the exhilaration of parachuting into an organization and magically "saving the day"—or at least illuminating dysfunction and offering practical, custom solutions. That is all great fun!

What goes into it, however, is not. In fact, much of that work sucks, to be blunt. Every hour spent playing the part of the genius in a workshop requires roughly a day of legwork spent alone or with my team, researching the organization, writing and organizing interactive questions, preparing "next steps" based on possible responses to those questions, creating slides and multimedia, and on and on. That work is tedious, rigorous, voluminous, and, at that moment, not particularly satisfying. I would do almost anything to get out of it.

But it is work that is necessary, so it gets done without excuses. I'm the "A" in my consultancy's name, "APS," and, as such, my participation and ideas are as important during planning as they are during execution—whether that be by me or one of my exceptional team. It's the most important part of the process—identifying problems and providing solutions—so I'm committed to it fully, each and every day.

I have complete faith in the team we've built and its ability to carry out this laborious preparation; not to mention the fact that I follow the smart person's guide to looking good—hiring people smarter than me! So I have a bountiful list of excuses I could make for leaving not just the drudgery but the nuanced solution-finding to them. The business and client list keep growing, so my strategic focus is required elsewhere. Prior to the COVID-19 pandemic, I was traveling a ridiculous amount, to the USA and EU from London twice a week at least. I need to devote time to our digital presence. I need to devote time to this book. The list goes on.

Surely, you have your own list of situation-specific excuses, in addition to those that are more general and forever at your disposal.

"I'm super busy."

This is the old standby—the cult of busy—where part of our worthiness as workers is wrapped up in being able to answer the question "How's it going?" with "I'm so busy," no matter who asks—your boss or a stranger on the train platform.

There are other excuses to accompany this one:

"I'm but a cog in the wheel."

"It's the fault of bureaucracy."

"It's always been done this way."

"I'm an extrovert, so it goes against my nature."

"I'm an introvert, so it goes against my nature."

Any of those statements may be true. But none of them should be offered as an excuse to avoid that which is unpleasant or difficult. None of them represent immovable barriers. And none are the statements of leaders. True leaders promise to reject excuses like these at every turn, even at the cost of their own comfort or personal gain.

By far the most prevalent excuse in the workplace is lack of time. It's the most widely deployed and the most readily accepted because collectively we've determined that being busy is a leading indicator of high performance. To be a true contributor, you must be really busy. You must cram your days with lots and lots of *stuff*. And you must ensure that others are aware of your busy-ness. When is the last time a colleague mentioned to you how busy they are? When is the last time you told someone how busy you are? Comparing notes on busy-ness has become standard workplace patter, as routine as noting the end of the week during an elevator ride:

"It's Friday."

"Yup. It's Friday."

"So busy."

"Yup. So busy."

Imagine if you asked a colleague how they've been and they responded, "I'm great! I'm progressing through tasks at a completely reasonable pace, and my inbox is well under control. I'm striking an ideal work–life balance, I'm getting eight hours of sleep, and I even have time to read 30 minutes before bed!" You would look at this person as if they were deranged. Worse than that, you might assume that this person is indolent and, failing that, lacking in ambition or simply not competent or capable enough to be appropriately "busy."

Feeling constantly and intensely busy—or at least saying that you are—is the new norm. And I'm not clear where this has come from. Is it a holdover from the Victorian workhouse ethic or an inevitable result of the growth of utilization cultures, where employees are left having to account for the organization's own take on the value of how you spend every moment of your working day.

I know some of you will have strict utilization targets that determine your appraisal rating, pay, and perception by bosses. You may feel forced to be "busy" every moment, destined to rise or fall in your organization by the amount and quality of "billable" time you spend.

So please know I see that you aren't "making up" you're busy, and please know that my team and I are working with employers to realize that utilization cultures are one of those elements of the old way of working that will not make it through to the future world of work—at least not as they exist now.

There are people in professional services, packing shelves in wholesale or retail environments for example, who need their scheduled breaks for physical and mental rest and who do rush from one task to another—they are legitimately "at capacity" and I think it's only fair to see that they might reject my blasé approach to the cult of busy. But I am still going to challenge you to embrace discomfort and not allow the short-sightedness of your employer to facilitate your personal stagnation.

We are mostly all busy. So it's not a distinguishing characteristic. And thus, it's a rubbish excuse. Nonetheless, I can't tell you how many times I hear some version of "Who's got the time?" Providing timely, actionable feedback? "Yes, I should. But who's got the time?" Empowering and elevating every voice on your team? "Sure, sounds lovely, but who's got the time?"

The demands of good leadership, productive collegiality, and, indeed, quality friendship are *not* about *more* time, but about time better spent.

Time is a precious and finite resource, yes. And I'm not suggesting that you magically create time out of thin air. But I am suggesting that you consider how you can change *how* you do what you do, even before you begin to think about how you might reassign time to achieve the results you want.

There are two things I would consider.

First, how might we be more focused, energized, and effective with the time that you have?

A few years ago, I did a video for kids in the UK who were thinking about attempting to deliver on their dream of playing professional basketball. I watched so many being industrious— working hard, doing variously effective "stuff," leaving the gym exhausted but not necessarily improved, and I wanted to share what I believe has propelled me in sport and in life after sport. I called it "Paying the FEE."

I am aware that people imagine success in any field is about innate physical, emotional, or cognitive talents, but my experience talking to high-achievers—and indeed my own life experience— tells me it is often more to do with an individual's ability to endure the mundanity of achieving success. The ability to tolerate the dull, uninspiring, painstaking planning. The willingness to enthusiastically embrace the repetitive, onerous, often physically and mentally taxing hours of practice so the eventual outcome or performance looks effortless.

FEE is an acronym for Focus, Effort and Execution:

• **Focus**—a single-minded, unwavering concentration on the creation of, and then progress toward, a clear, discrete, and well-defined target or goal

- **Effort**—the discipline to apply yourself to mundane, vexing, or obscure tasks and preparation with consistent eagerness and enthusiasm

- **Execution**—undertaking everything you do with the goal of eliminating unnecessary variance so that everything you do is not just effortful but done to a tight tolerance based on your plan.

People think that "personal industry" alone is enough to be successful, but unfortunately, it's just not enough in this disrupted world where equality of opportunity has no guarantees. There is a personal indulgence many of us engage in, where we never really push ourselves to know our limits. People suffer from Parkinson's Law (the adage that "work expands so as to fill the time available for its completion"), and as such people can make themselves remarkably "busy" without ever actually being stretched beyond their comfort level—without ever even approaching their actual capacity for delivery of key outcomes.

The one advantage of visible, frenetic activity is that it gives all of us the excuses to abandon the so-called "nice to have" stuff involved in being a true colleague, teammate and leader that would allow us to reach our true potential.

Watch the video at https://vimeo.com/133266894 (please don't be alarmed, but the video is old and there will be no big, white beard in sight!) and then consider how you might—with all the real constraints in your life—pay the FEE a little more effectively.

The second thing to do when considering your time and how you spend it is to appreciate what any person—what you—can do with just a little time.

My mother was the first person to teach me the power of time used with presence and purpose—a lesson that has shaped my whole life.

My mum, you'll recall, was a general practitioner in Stockport in the 1970s. When I was seven, I would accompany her on house visits, mostly because my sisters and I would quarrel if left home alone. But I did not look forward to these outings. Mum regularly treated patients in palliative care—patients who were in grave condition and were not going to get better. So I spent lots of time in houses where the heaviness of grief made it difficult to breathe. I remember telling my mother that, when we walked into those homes, it felt like something was "squashing" my chest.

We would usually be greeted at the door by a family member who would usher us to the living room before leading my mother to the patient in another room. I would sit with the family, waiting for Mum to return. Sometimes it was just me and one other person, and other times the room was packed. But there is one sound I associate with all of those visits: the nervous clinking and tinkling of a teacup on a saucer. Back then, when doctors came round for house visits, families made sure to set out their best bone china. So, once settled in the living room, I'd be handed a cup and saucer. And everyone else in the room would have their cup and saucer. And together we'd wait, breathing in that heavy air; silent aside from the unsettling tinnitus of teacup rattling on saucer. Unsteady hands, trembling with distress and fear.

After a few minutes, my mother would finish her work and come back to the living room. And regardless of what instructions or diagnosis she needed to deliver, she would first pause in the doorway as if surveying the room, saying not a word. She did this quite deliberately, making eye contact with each person as if scooping them all up into her attention, ensuring they knew they were her singular priority during this time together.

Once seated, she would let the family air their worries and concerns, and some would be despondent while others were hysterical. "We can't cope, Dr. Amaechi," they'd say, often through tears. "How can we possibly manage this? Nothing can be done, we are overwhelmed, we are devastated! How will we go on?"

By now, Mum would have a bone china saucer and teacup of her own. Once everyone had gotten their chance to speak, she would scan the room again. And with a rock-solid delivery—not a sound from her teacup or saucer—she would look in their eyes and calmly say, "You *can* do this. You're *going* to do this."

And they would sometimes push back: "But no, Dr. Amaechi, you don't understand ..."

"No," she would insist. "You can do this. And you are going to do this." Almost always, her words of assurance were accompanied by a slight hand gesture, the slightest wave of a relaxed hand—fingers, spread just enough to catch the swirling doubts and fear.

Then, with a serene self-assuredness, she would assign each person a task to carry them forward. This is what you are going to do over the next seven days to support your loved one and the rest of the family.

"That is how you'll get through, and I'll be back to see you in a week. You can do this."

The effect of her words was profound. Almost immediately the air would lighten and you could breathe easier. The hands steadied, and the bone china went quiet. It wasn't that Mum had delivered their beloved back to health. But, in these moments, it was as if she had brought the family back to life. Using only a few words, delivered with cool confidence and genuine care, she would reignite the resolve of an entire family that only minutes earlier had been paralyzed and exhausted by sorrow.

"Yes, Dr. Amaechi," someone would repeat back. "You're right. We can do this. We will do this and this and this. And we'll see you in a week." I was always struck by the verbatim accuracy with which the families would recount what my mum had "prescribed" for each of them to help them cope.

I was blown away by my mother's power during these brief episodes—her ability to transform the dynamic of the gathering, to inspire hope in a truly hopeless situation. It was hard for a seven-year-old to fully comprehend—I just knew it was magic.

I know I was seven because I know it was 1977. And I know it was 1977 because, after one of these outings with Mum, she took me to the cinema for what would be a life-altering event: the release of the first *Star Wars* film, retrospectively titled *A New Hope*.

By that time, I was obsessively reading science fiction and clearly on the fast track to both geek- and nerd-dom. Those magnificent gold words on the inky background of space were a gateway to another dimension. "A long time ago in a galaxy far, far away ..."

Once the intro text started crawling, I was gone, consumed by that incredible world that seemed so distant from reality—weird robots and stormtroopers scurrying about space and some heavy-breathing super-villain harassing a princess with weird buns. I didn't know where I was, but I was enthralled.

About 43 minutes 30 seconds in (42 minutes 30 seconds in the original version!), though, that extraordinary fantasy universe suddenly seemed strangely familiar. That's when Obi-Wan Kenobi and Luke Skywalker are cruising through the Mos Eisley space-port on their way to the Cantina, and they're stopped by a patrol of stormtroopers who are looking for some droids matching the description of R2-D2 and C-3PO. I remember being quite confused watching this scene, wondering how it could possibly play out in favor of our heroes. The droids were obvious and in plain view, stretched out in the back of Luke's landspeeder—an inescapable bind, it would seem. Maybe *Star Wars* would be a really short movie with a baffling ending?

The stormtroopers start interrogating Luke, prying into his ownership history with the droids and demanding that he show some ID. But Uncle Obi-Wan is unfazed. He's sitting shotgun, left elbow propped on the door frame, cool as a cucumber, the hood of his casual Jedi robe slung over his head. He looks at the stormtrooper with a serious, gentle gaze and says, "You don't need to see his identification."

Whoa.

The stormtrooper hesitates a split second and then obediently repeats back, "We don't need to see his identification."

Whoa!

"These aren't the droids you're looking for," Obi-Wan says.

"These aren't the droids we're looking for," the stormtrooper replies. And then, again parroting Obi-Wan's words, the stormtrooper instructs Luke to "go about his business." Despite the fact that the droids are *right there*!

I had seen this before, something very similar. I missed the next several minutes of the film, so completely distracted was I, staring at the side of my mum's face in wonder and running through the memories of every living room we'd visited. I recognized the economy of words. The conviction of delivery. The intensity of focus. The power of it all. I had seen this! Every time my mother altered moods and behaviors with just a few words and her undivided attention, that must have been the Force! How else to explain it? As if on cue, my mother reached for the popcorn. And noticing my look of revelation, she raised her right eyebrow (a trait thankfully passed down from mother to son) and gave a knowing smile and nod that to me said, "Exactly!" In hindsight, that look could have meant anything or nothing. But in the moment it was definite confirmation that my mum was a Jedi.

The implications of this possibility grew as the movie continued, hinting at genetic links to the Force. By the closing credits, I was convinced that I, too, would become a Jedi. Perhaps Mum had not shared this because I was not "of age"—still too young to fully understand. Luke was much older than I, after all, and even he seemed rather naïve on the matter.

After the movie, I was burning for answers. But I decided not to ask Mum about it directly. Instead, I would do some preliminary research at our local library (I told you I was a nerd), where I was a near-daily visitor anyway. On my next visit, I rushed up to the circulation desk, and, bypassing pleasantries with the lone staff member, explained what my mum did in those patient's houses and demanded to be directed toward the books about "becoming a Jedi."

"Well, the *Star Wars* books are over …" the librarian started to answer, but I cut her off almost immediately.

"No, no, you misunderstand me." I placed both hands on the desk, very dramatic. "I don't need books about the film. I need books about how one *becomes a Jedi*."

She was not getting it. So I explained further, speaking as clearly and as slowly as any excited and impatient seven-year-old can. I matter-of-factly explained what my mum did in her patients' homes—how the air went from heavy to light, how people listened and repeated back exactly what she said ...

There is a great chance that this librarian knew my mum—everyone did—and this library was directly next door to my mum's surgery ... so she may have been my mum's patient. Either way, she eventually understood something at the core of my ask.

The librarian was very patient and said my description sounded a bit like "psychology." Perhaps that would be of interest? I was not familiar with the word but was raring to go. Plus, it was entirely possible she was in on Mum's secret too and didn't want to be direct. "You can call it whatever you like," I said. "Direct me to the literature on 'psychology.'" She pointed the way.

For a couple hours, I sat on the library floor reading grown-up books about psychology. It was ultimately an introduction to my eventual vocation. But at the time I was thinking only about power. The Force. Being special. I wanted to be like my mother and Obi-Wan. I wanted to impact people the way my mum did. I wanted to be a Jedi.

These were childish thoughts, not only because the Force is a fictional concept, but because I was chasing a set of capabilities that I've since learned exist in everyone. I had a misconception that the Force was reserved for Jedi or doctors or psychologists—an elite few. That is wrong, though. There are degrees of scale, but we all share Jedi potential—it's will, commitment, and discipline that separate the Jedi (or Sith) from the rest ...

In a world where technology is rapidly displacing in-person connections and placing at risk authentic connections, the gift of your undivided attention—however fleeting—is increasingly valuable. I tell my colleagues all the time that your attention is a weapon. It's a strange weapon in that its absence is what is guaranteed to wound others.

You cannot be too busy to withhold it. If we're honest about it, we know we choose when we are too busy, often on the basis of whether the person we might invest time with can do something for us or not, or whether they are senior to us.

It's an investment of seconds in some cases. Take the ending of in-person meetings, for example. When attendees disperse, how do you spend the walk back to your desk? Do you use that fleeting time to thank the presenter for her work or to ask a question or to offer a tip or suggestion? Do you use it to check in with a familiar colleague and ask how their family's been? Do you introduce yourself to a fellow attendee whom you hadn't previously met? Even when virtual those same commitments of time can come in the form of an email of thanks, an offer of support, or a texted suggestion of a way to be even better.

These acts are not just courtesies. Every second of your time and attention can be powerful because *you are powerful*. And denying that second truth is just another way of making an excuse to avoid the inconvenience of using that power and that time to good effect.

Too many people in this world try to escape the responsibility of their power by pretending that it doesn't exist. And there is nothing more dangerous to an organization than powerful people who refuse to accept that they wield any power at all—not because of any fear of their own influence, but because of the accompanying, inevitable responsibility to be uncomfortable that power necessitates.

Denial of status may be deployed as an excuse when you can't fight the temptation to indulge in frivolous gossip or workplace politics. What's the harm if you talk a little smack or a joke at someone's expense? It's only coming from "little ol' you"! You can be "down," right? Wrong. Respect and understand your power, even when it means the discomfort of missing out on some cheap fun.

Each of us must accept that our merest gaze—a casual glance in someone's direction—has an impact. Unless you're alone, looking angry will have an impact on others. You can *be* irritated for any number of reasons, sure. But you can't carry it on your face as you wait at the elevators. You can't slip an eye roll during a video conference or take that walk back to your desk with a clenched jaw and the veins in your temple pulsing. Innocent bystanders will absorb that irritation or, worse, they will wonder if they are the source—especially for those of you who are influential or named leaders in your organizations.

"It's only little ol' me" can't be an excuse. That's not an excuse for tuning out your colleagues in favor of your phone during a conversation. "It's only the weekly staff meeting." That doesn't justify skimming emails while others are talking.

Remember, there are no pivotal moments. Nothing you do is so routine that *how* you do it stops being important, impactful, or even game-changing. Something being routine doesn't mean how you do it becomes inconsequential, and believing otherwise is one of the ways we justify the avoidance of effort and discomfort in those moments. This isn't an indictment of you—human beings are evolutionarily wired to be lazy, to conserve energy. It was a survival strategy.

True leaders get this right. So do true colleagues and friends.

They don't operate on the idea that attention or interest among their people fluctuates or that there are peaks and lulls in the need for connection. True leaders promise their A game at all times because they know that, by being who they are, even humdrum, seemingly trivial engagement can be transformative.

Think about the "routine" meetings you lead and attend where topics might be discussed in which you're already well versed. Meetings where decisions might be bandied about long after you've decided you know what's best. It's far easier to plow through these onerous meetings and finish a few minutes early than it is to participate in a truly collaborative meeting. Collaborative, inclusive meetings risk the introduction of alternative viewpoints and even additional work. But they also lead to better results—to winning, both in the present and the future. They prepare you and your team for the occasions when you *won't* have all the answers, when you need their collective input and expertise.

Such meetings are far more energy expensive. So when possible, it's tempting to go the quick-and-easy route and tell yourself that it's just another meeting. You've been doing this a long time, after all. You don't know exactly what's on the horizon, but it's probably not much different than what you've already seen and known, right? Certainly, nothing that requires immediate attention. So what's the harm in breezing through a meeting, when there's so much on your plate and you just don't have the energy today? It won't make a difference in the long run. That's what you'll tell yourself, at least. That will be your rationalization.

"It won't make a difference" is an extension of the previously mentioned excuses but one that can also be used on its own. This is the convenient idea that you can take a shortcut on occasion because, at the end of the day, forces beyond your control are guiding the ship. So, if the process is broken, the system is rigged, and we're all merely players on a stage where higher powers pull the strings, then how can you make a difference?

We point to massive structural challenges—organizational design, remuneration structures, minority recruiting, career development, strategic objectives, clumsy processes and more— and throw our hands in the air. If critical matters like these are neglected or mismanaged from on high, we say, then whatever we do at ground level won't amount to a hill of beans, right? Wrong. Again, a handy rationalization. But completely wrong.

Individual contributions and behaviors drive culture. Focusing on faulty infrastructure or an incompetent bureaucracy allows us to stand in solidarity with our colleagues and point to an external problem that is not our fault. And that can be comforting. But it's not very useful. What can you do? What actions can you take to build trust, resilience, and innovation? Systems and process be damned, how can *you* make a difference, no matter how small?

It is important to recognize that there are elements around us beyond our control—places where bureaucracy or process hampers thriving, but often we see people use these elements that are legitimately out of their control to ratify their inaction in areas that are categorically *within* it. This is a self-indulgent excuse that spreads like a virus infecting others with apathy in the face of opportunity—all just to avoid putting ourselves out, to avoid discomfort.

We're in a very different world right now, and, despite what you may have been told, there is no new normal. It's likely that you will have to do things differently than you've done them before. You might have to flex a bit in ways that do not feel comfortable, and while I am encouraging discomfort, it comes with rewards and doesn't mean abandoning self-care. Each of us must learn that point where functional discomfort—which supports friends or colleagues and enables personal and organizational performance—gives way to pain—which signals a need to take more time for yourself. Self-care is not eliminated by embracing discomfort; it is prioritized and reframed as something to continually monitor and schedule into your life so that you have the resources at other times to embrace the discomfort of really showing up for your team and your dreams.

The avoidance of discomfort can manifest in the most mundane of ways.

How often do you hear someone struggle to recall a name and rationalize it by saying, "I have the worst memory!" or "I'm terrible with names!"?

You *may* have a bad memory, but it cannot be an excuse for not knowing the names of the people you work with. There are so-called leaders who walk by the same colleagues every day without acknowledging them by name, leaning on the broadly accepted excuse that remembering names is difficult, especially when you're an important person with lots of other stuff to remember.

And it's rubbish! If they truly wanted to remember the receptionist's name, they would figure out a way to remember the receptionist's name, just like they figure out ways to remember the names of the myriad of important clients, customers, and board members. Having a "bad memory" cannot be an excuse.

Being an introvert cannot be an excuse, as much as I wish it could be. As an extreme introvert myself, I find it exhausting to be around people for long stretches of time. This may seem to contradict my earlier sentiment about the thrill and reward of hands-on client interaction. But it's not; both are true. To meet my own goals and those of my company, APS, I need to engage with other humans to an extent that can feel unwelcome in the moment, but essential and, in the end, epically worthwhile.

My instinct in those group situations is to retreat—to find a quiet place and curl up into a ball. But I am committed to the energy expenditure because the reward is amazing. I work through the introversion and flex beyond my comfort zone because the win is worth it.

Natural extroverts may need to flex in the opposite direction to temper their impulses. Being an extrovert does not justify interrupting colleagues, stepping on their words while shoving yours to the forefront. It does not excuse behavior that is reminiscent of Ricky Gervais in *The Office*. And it certainly does not excuse inappropriate "banter." Being a type-A people person—an "open book" who is comfortable in all settings and quick to engage— is wonderful. But it is not a free pass to act without restraint. I occasionally meet men who fail to grasp this. Men who resent, for example, the expectation that they refrain from making observations about their coworkers' appearances. "Who doesn't love a compliment?" they contend. They're not predators, and they think they should not be censored or prohibited just because others might make similar comments with more sinister intent. They're extroverts, they argue, this is how they are! And what's the harm in telling the receptionist he looks lovely today? Everyone loves being told they look lovely!

It's not true. Rein it in. Even if that means you don't get to be your fully extroverted self.

Being a great leader and a great colleague requires you to flex. It requires you to sometimes act in ways that do not feel comfortable. How do you respond in the face of discomfort? Do you act with resolve and do the necessary work? Or do you dip into your reliable inventory of excuses?

Unfortunately, in my experience, I've found that most influential or senior leaders and many tenured colleagues have a tension that they resolve poorly where impending discomfort is a possibility. This happens to some of the best-known and ostensibly successful people and organizations in the world. When faced with a challenge, they prioritize comfort—or at least the avoidance of personal discomfort—over organizational performance or their own long-term goals.

That's what real success is about, though—a relentless focus, effort, and execution, even when a less effortful option may be "good enough." Organizational hurdles are not usually cleared by sudden infusions of funding or overhauls of the business structure. It is the individual actions of named and unnamed leaders—the energy that they're willing to expend, their tolerance for personal discomfort, their rejection of excuses, and their dismissal of self-interest. That is what fuels change.

A few years ago at the London Marathon, there was a viral moment that perfectly illustrated this promise in action. David Wyeth was an amateur competitor and a member of the Chorlton Runners club, and this was not his first marathon. He had completed a few prior and with respectable times. But at this particular event something went awry. With a few thousand yards left in the race, David's body appeared to be shutting down. It was difficult to watch. His gait was reduced to a crablike hobble as if he was trapped in a dream where the body refuses to respond to the brain's direction; his feet looked heavy as concrete.

At this very last stage of the race, the course bends hard to the right, leading to the homestretch and a clear view of the finish line, only a couple hundred yards away. David had no chance of making it; that seemed clear. As the other runners made the turn to the right, he staggered along straight ahead, slowly straying from the pack and struggling to get one foot ahead of the other. The spectator footage of this on YouTube is quite dramatic. You hear the concern of onlookers and Wagner's "Ride of the Valkyries" pumping out of loudspeakers stationed in the shadows of Buckingham Palace. And poor David Wyeth is drifting farther and farther to the left like a crippled animal that should be put out of its misery.

All the while, the other runners are cruising by. Literally, hundreds pass this broken man without breaking pace. Among them are fellow amateurs raising money for charities that support people in medical crisis. None of them slows down for the medical emergency that is evolving before their eyes. And yes, it is likely that some of them don't see David or that, after 26 miles, a few of them are not in a condition to assist. But, by and large, people consciously blow past him, sometimes doing him the favor of shouted encouragement as they pass. Keeping his stride, one gentleman gives David a thumbs-up and a hearty pat on the back that looks like it might just knock him over.

Also among the runners is Matthew Rees, a banker and amateur runner with the Swansea Harriers club. We learn later that he's been fighting a cramp in his calf since the start of the race and has given up on trying to achieve a personal best. But, closing in on the turn, he realizes that, with a bit more speed, he'll be able to finish just over his personal best. Not too shabby. Accelerating his pace, though, Matthew spots David—a complete stranger, representing a different running club. And Matthew does what no one else saw fit to do: he stops.

"It was not a decision," he says later. "When I saw him struggling, that was that. I was going to help him. I didn't want him running 26 miles for a steward to pull him out and not make the final 200 meters."

David does not make it easy for Matthew to help. He's struggling to stay on his feet when Matthew approaches, but he has just enough energy to resist, weakly waving him away with one flailing arm. I'm fine, he's telling him, I've got this. Please go finish your race. Matthew stands his ground. His determination to help is remarkable. But David is fading fast and soon collapses to the pavement. The other runners continue to pass. At no point does anyone else slow down.

Matthew helps David back to his feet and points to the finish line, which is now in sight. "You can do it! You will finish," he demands. "I won't leave your side. We'll get to that finish line."

David is wobbly but upright, supported by Matthew's arm around his waist. The pair start a slow march to the finish line, and for the first time another runner stops to offer help! But the barely lucid David waves him off, and the runner, unlike Matthew, assents, proceeding about his way. All it took for him to eschew responsibility was the limp wave of a desperate man who could neither think nor see straight. That is all the excuse that runner needed to return his attention to his own self-interest. *Need help, clearly incapacitated person? Nope? Alrighty then, see you at the finish line!*

Matthew Rees accepted no excuses despite their availability. If he'd passed David like hundreds of others did, no one would've noticed. Matthew had no obligation to the man or the Chorlton Runners. He had his own calf pain to contend with. He had a personal goal to finish under 2 hours 50 minutes. And whether he stopped or not probably wouldn't matter in the long run. He could be reasonably confident that David would not drop dead on the course. Someone would do something, right? There are people at marathons whose job it is to do something. So eventually someone would do something. Matthew had plenty of excuses to justify not stopping, and he rejected them all with hardly a thought.

Eventually, a race official joins the pair to support David from the other side. At this point, Matthew was no longer needed, and he could have probably still finished under 2 hours 50 minutes by leaving David safely behind. But he did not. He saw it through to the end. And the three of them staggered to the finish line, with other runners passing by and occasionally giving one or the other a pat on the back. That was their contribution. That was their version of doing something.

When David, Matthew, and the official finally cross the finish line, Matthew casually peels away from the group, replaced by the waiting medical staff. He checks his watch. He has not finished under 2:50. He does not seem bothered.

"I can't say how grateful I am to Matthew," David says in remarks after the marathon in an interview they did together for *The Guardian* newspaper. "You say, Matthew, that others would have stopped. And I'm sure you're right. There may have been others, but ... you persisted. I told you to go, and you still didn't."

In Matthew Rees' comments, he says that, despite not achieving a personal best, crossing the line with David Wyeth was a perfect ending. True leaders understand this—that the rewards of mutual success and shared vision will always outweigh those of individual accomplishment.

In the televised broadcast of the Rees–Wyeth finish, the commentators are joined in the booth by world-class endurance runner James Cracknell, who has already finished the race. James is a two-time Olympic gold medalist in rowing, and his observations show a champion's appreciation for Matthew Rees' selflessness. More interesting, though, is the regret that James expresses over his own decisions during the race.

"I saw a couple of people in real trouble," he says. "And I gave them a pat on the bum when I ran past and said 'keep going' rather than stop and help them along. So I'm feeling slightly guilty and selfish, having watched other people give up their race to help someone who's just emptied their tanks totally."

You can hear a hint of shame in James' voice, an acknowledgment that, on this day, he finished with an elite time but failed to meet the true standard of a champion. Matthew met that standard. To the detriment of his own performance and despite a host of available excuses, he took action. He had no reason to believe that this selflessness would be noticed, much less publicized and lauded. But he took action all the same.

This is *The Promises of Giants*. That we will do right by people— care for, protect, and develop them—every step of the way, even when it is not in our own immediate interest and even when it is uncomfortable or difficult. If you keep this promise, I am confident that you'll learn what Matthew Rees and James Cracknell know to be true. The short-term pain and inconvenience of individual sacrifice are well worth the collective long-term rewards.

Whether you're a giant, a Jedi, a named or unnamed leader, an Olympic champion or an anonymous amateur, your decisions have the power. There is no acceptable discomfort or justifiable excuse for acting otherwise.

CHAPTER 6

I Promise to Tend to Mind and Body

My brain just works better when I move.

I work out four or five times a week—usually lifting three mornings and some "easy" Yin Yoga to stretch my body out at the end of a day I have usually spent staring into three computer screens.

I will admit that I quite enjoy Yin Yoga, but I hate lifting—I hated it when I was a pro athlete and I hate it now I am the opposite of a pro athlete. However, the combination of strength work and stretching helps my brain to work more effectively and for longer and helps me be the kind of leader and teammate for my colleagues and problem-solver for our clients that I need to be and that they rightly expect.

This last self-directed promise stands to benefit you more immediately than any promise in the book. But, in this context, even the promise to tend to your own mind and body is not just about you. It's about ensuring the sustainability of your own internal resources because your attention, patience, energy and more will be taxed in order for you to achieve your goals and be relied upon by others in your business and social circles. Not to mention the fact that exhibiting responsible self-care behaviors sets a positive example for others.

It's no secret that we are living in times characterized by change, disruption, and unprecedented pressure to innovate in order to thrive—from geopolitical crises to global pandemics, we are having more asked of us physically and psychologically than we might have considered possible. This applies to us as individuals within organizations and to the organizations themselves among a field of competitors. But you cannot hope to effectively lead others to sustained success if you're neglecting the needs of your own wellbeing. The following maxim is one I love and is truer now than ever:

"You can't pour from an empty cup."

The ability to lead through disruption is vital. But the ability to do so while being mindful of your personal wellbeing and that of your colleagues will be a differentiator. Your mindset and your habits have an immediate impact, not only on your own wellbeing but on that of the people around you.

First, I want to address the concept of resilience. I think most people think it means the ability to endure and bounce back from a "setback" or some kind of generic adversity. When used this way I like the idea of resilience. However, it's important to note that it takes time to cultivate this kind of fortitude. Be suspicious of anyone who tries to sell you "success in five minutes"—instantaneous change is unrealistic.

If someone is running up a hill to reach a goal, there is a weight you can reasonably ask them to carry alone and assume that their pace and endurance will be unaffected. Then there are weights that you might expect the runner to be able to manage, but only at a reduced pace and for a shorter distance. The runner carrying this second, heavier weight, is resilient, but in order to complete the task safely, the runner and their team must adjust their expectations. Both of these weights might be considered "adversity," but while the first weight does not require the runner to make any changes, the second example requires accommodations in order for the runner to complete the task safely.

However, there are also weights where we might imagine it possible for a person to carry the burden alone for a moment but where any reasonable person would understand it would be inadvisable due to the risk of permanent harm and long-term durability, as well as, indeed, due the ethical imperative that is our duty of care for each other.

Early resilience research focused on resilience as the ability to overcome trauma—not just adversity—and this, with the help of popular interpretations, encouraged people to think that resilience is about invulnerability.

It is not.

The importance of wellbeing and its relevance to the workplace may not be universally accepted, but it has been more fulsomely embraced in part because of the disruptions we have recently endured from Black Lives Matter to COVID-19.

However, there are likely some people reading this who instinctively recoil from the mention of a phrase like "mind and body," especially after a chapter on embracing discomfort! This skepticism or outright dismissal is particularly common among more grizzled and hardened veterans of work and life—people who supposedly have had it much tougher than these young "snowflakes" and who view the misery they endured as a necessary rite of passage.

There is a kernel of truth here. Generations upon generations of workers, particularly in highly competitive industries, have been treated terribly. And career advancement has largely been dependent upon the ability to withstand terrible treatment (aka trauma) for long periods of time.

Nurturing and developing a workforce, establishing a positive corporate culture—these are relatively new priorities and in most industries still very much a work in progress. Much of today's corporate elite was shaped by managers who were never part of that environment and would have had little interest in a book like this. They existed in a world where any number of sins were ignored or forgiven. But, broadly speaking, they could treat people like crap and run them into the ground on the at best dubious philosophy that "whatever doesn't kill you makes you stronger."

And thus they produced a cohort of descendants—today's leaders—who survived and thrived and attribute their success largely to the struggle. They equate pain with growth, concluding that, because they endured an awful experience, it made them a great leader. So to be a great leader, others must be open to awful experiences. You can sympathize with this rationalization to an extent. If people did not believe that their "rite of passage" was directly tied to their success, they would be left with a less inspiring reality: they were just being treated like crap. That is closer to the truth. You can, of course, learn from negative experiences. But, in almost all cases, positive or neutral experiences can teach the same lessons. You don't have to be beaten up at school to learn resilience skills.

I've mentioned all this upfront to ensure that when I reference resilience, it does not mean indomitable, it does not mean invulnerable, and it does not imply that you can continue at the same pace and for the same amount of time without breaking something important.

My brain works better when I move. I know exactly how to push myself a little more in every class to feel a sense of growth and accomplishment, but not so much that I am negatively impacted by muscle strains and actual pain the next day. And I also recognize those days when I need to take a break, even from exercise, in the interests of an even greater good.

The promise to tend to body and mind is not about coddling or pampering yourself or others. It's not a promise that you're going to stop working hard. Again, we tend to be selective in the marginal gains that we value. We make this promise because marginal gains made in the area of self-care pay off exponentially in overall productivity and effectiveness. We also make it because marginal gains has a wicked stepsister: diminishing returns. Many of our workplaces have become 24/7 operations, whether deliberately or not. Technology has eroded boundaries and allowed us to be accessible after hours and on the weekends. And while there may be some value to that availability, it is limited or negated altogether by the harm done by constantly being "on." You can push yourself and others only so far before you start to compromise, even without knowing it.

There are obviously more exhaustive resources available to you that focus exclusively on wellbeing. But, in the context of leadership, there are seven factors of individual resilience that demand our attention and directly contribute to sustained high performance.

1 A healthy mindset

This may be the greatest determinant of success and is certainly responsible for much of the variance in achievement between those with similar IQs, experience, and work ethics.

Of late, mindfulness has emerged as a trendy lifestyle concept. But the ability to fix your mind entirely in the present moment is an essential precursor to success and happiness. If you can't focus on your chosen cognitive processes and perceptions, the world will always be a confusing cacophony. And, for many of us, it is!

Practicing mindfulness is not easy in a world where the pace is breakneck and competition for attention is fierce; in a world where "multitasking" is considered a necessary skill despite piles of evidence indicating it's actually counterproductive—akin to tabbed browsing in its effectiveness and its drag on processing speed.

A healthy mindset allows for objective filtering of what is real and what is imagined, what is useful and what is useless. What are the stories that we tell ourselves all day, and what does the voice sound like? Is it overly critical? Unhelpful? Accurate, even? Here again, we see the value of the Effective Feedback Model (see Chapter 1). Challenging our inner narrator through those questions sharpens perspective. And if you do it consistently and deliberately, it will soon become habitual and second nature. It will also inform and improve your "control orientation." This is the ability to identify and embrace that which you control and to avoid fixating on that which you don't. "Control the controllable"—because that is all you can do.

Finally, where mindset is concerned, take an honest assessment of where you stand on the spectrum between "growth" and "fixed." Do you have a fixed mindset, constrained by a sense that your own intelligence and talent, as well as that of others, are innate and immutable? Is your ambition tempered by the risk of failure? The fear of what is beyond your capacity? Or do you approach the world with a growth mindset? Confident that, with effort, people are generally able to expand their knowledge and acquire new skills? Are you open to making mistakes and to the growth opportunities that accompany occasional failure?

The benefits of viewing ourselves through the lens of a growth mindset should be obvious. It liberates us from the demands of perfection. It invites us to be vulnerable and extend beyond our comfort zone. It encourages a kind of flexibility that allows us to roll with the tides of change and to innovate through difficult circumstances and encourages us to look for ways—even small ones—to expand our understanding and integrate new learnings from success or failure into our insights and strategies for the future.

But where personal wellbeing is concerned, it is critical that leaders also apply a growth mindset toward how they view others. You cannot do it all. You cannot win alone. And that means you will need to believe in and rely upon your team and colleagues, perhaps in ways that are not always comfortable. You will need to take some leaps of faith and trust in the abilities and potential of those who surround you. Effective delegation requires a growth mindset, and it will be virtually impossible for you to evolve and reach your goals without delegating.

2 Active learning

Of course, having a mindset that is enthusiastic toward learning is only the foundation. The second factor that contributes to resilience is the actual act of learning. Humans are pre-programmed to gather information, seek out new discoveries, and acquire skills. But that instinct is often suppressed by the demands on our time and the temptation to settle for "good enough" when we are stressed or tired. In the face of long hours and longer to-do lists, it seems onerous to consider taking on more. But devoting time to reading, developing your talents, and experimenting with new skills—related to work or not—will likely make you a more content, tranquil, and well-rounded person.

3 Balanced nutrition

It's a simple fact that, when time is short and pressure is high, our dietary decisions are made based on convenience rather than what our body needs. And, for many of us, when stress is added into the equation, we choose food that is not only convenient but also reassuring, if only for a fleeting moment. Prioritizing what your body needs for optimal performance is essentially a matter of discipline—investing the time to plan how you will nourish yourself, even on days when your schedule is filled with a gauntlet of back-to-back-to-back meetings.

Beyond that general point of taking the time to eat well, there are a few dietary goals that everyone should be able to meet. First, appreciate the necessity of breakfast. It is a vital meal that the body demands to literally break the fast that it has endured overnight. Coffee is not a breakfast. A banana is barely a breakfast. Starting your morning with a balanced and nutritious meal will improve your mental state throughout the day and is a habit that should not be undervalued.

Second, drink water. Lots of it. As with the advice to eat breakfast, this is not rocket science and likely not the first time you're hearing it. But dehydration is scientifically proven to lower IQ! As little as four hours without a glass of water will start to affect brain structure and cognitive function, even in otherwise fit and healthy adults.

And, lastly, refrain from using your schedule as an excuse for poor dietary habits. And certainly do not do this publicly. How often have you heard someone say they haven't eaten all day? The subtext here is that what they've instead been doing is very important—all-consuming, even. And people who do very important, all-consuming things must sometimes sacrifice feeding their body.

Bollocks.

Do not say this aloud, much less with any degree of pride. It is a poor reflection of your priorities. But, worse, it is poor modeling. It sets an expectation that leadership and advancement will sometimes come at the expense of personal health and wellbeing. If you are going to skip lunch, do not further the damage by sharing that poor decision as if it were an honorable act of duty.

4 Physical activity

While competitive sport is not for everyone, the evidence for simple movement helping the body and mind is overwhelming. An exercise routine comprised of a brisk 30-minute walk alone has been shown to improve heart and lung fitness, reduce anxiety, and elevate mood and energy. So, whether you are simply walking an extra stop to the station during your daily commute or you're exerting more energy by taking a community bike for a spin on the weekend or joining a Zumba class, you are strengthening the body and creating space for the mind to relax and peacefully mull over challenges in the background—a state that is ideal for generating breakthrough "eureka" moments.

5 Occasional pauses

Just as important as this basic act of doing something is the basic act of doing nothing! The fifth factor of resilience is taking moments to just … pause. Too many high performers spend their lives "buried in the red line," and that is not sustainable in the long term. Previously, when discussing how the time immediately after a meeting could be used, I warned against walking through your office in a harried manner that suggests you do not wish to be disturbed. That remains sound advice. However, it does not mean that you need to be constantly and absolutely available to people at all times.

It is important that you find ways to pause in the course of a day. A momentary change in pace, posture, or pursuit operates like a gear change that allows a perceptible increase in pace after the lull. So find a way to deliberately disconnect from your screens and the noise that surrounds you, if only for a few minutes each day. You will find that these quick "resets" make you better at your job when you continue. For the price of 10 minutes spread throughout the day, the performance dividend of a pause is exponential.

6 Consistent recuperation

The big-picture version of pausing is recuperation. Sports scientists are increasingly finding that active and strategic recuperation following games and practice is the key to extending careers. But you are not Lebron James or Marcus Rashford, so we're not talking about compression pants or cryotherapy chambers. Nor are we talking about napping or kicking back on the couch. Recuperation in this context is, in the knowledge of your personality and temperament, finding moments in your schedule to do things that recharge and reenergize you. For some, this is a trip to the gym. For others, it's reading for pleasure. But, whether it's a quiet, solitary walk in the woods or joining friends for a night of live music, find a recuperative activity and invest time into it at least once a week. Recuperation is almost never simply the act of passing out through exhaustion when all your mandated tasks are done. That's the path to burnout and waking up feeling ever less refreshed.

7 A good night's sleep

Lastly, do not sleep on the importance of sleep! It is our final factor and a bedrock for resilience. No one is programmed to be an optimal performer with fewer than six hours of quality sleep. And here again, as with diet, if you insist upon neglecting sleep in favor of work, at least limit the damage by not modeling that behavior—even if it means that you save those late-night emails as drafts and send them the next morning. Competing to see who can function with the least sleep runs counter to a true high-performance narrative.

Some of you may have difficulty sleeping, and, if that is the case, you need to work on it. Falling asleep is a skill like any other. Establish an end-of-day routine—a set of to-dos for the last hour of wakefulness that starts with routine and necessary tasks (e.g., ironing shirts or preparing the next day's lunch) and ends with relaxing and enjoyable (but not overstimulating) activities. This routine need not include your phone or television. Sleep time should be synonymous with a reduction of stimuli and arousal. Minimizing exposure to stimuli such as social media or the nightly news is critical for finding the proper frame of mind for a restorative night's sleep.

These seven factors for resilience—a healthy mindset, active learning, balanced nutrition, physical activity, occasional pauses, consistent recuperation, and a good night's sleep—are not particularly complicated. The ability to manage your mind and body with care is not beyond the capacity of anyone reading this book. And, in that regard, this promise is consistent with those you've been asked to make to yourself already. Harness the power of introspection to see yourself clearly. Commit fully to winning and all that it requires. Be bold yet vulnerable. Act with vigilance against biases. Reject excuses and embrace discomfort.

Before we proceed further, I'd like to challenge you to review and consider all that we've discussed to this point. And then take a moment, with all of that in mind, to commit to making one change. Just one. It can be something you stop doing or something you start doing, as long as it's one change that progresses you toward being your best self, your best giant. Then, once you've committed to that change, take whatever steps may be necessary to clear your path and ensure that you make good on your commitment. That's the precommitment work—eliminating obstacles, neutralizing temptations, and constructing conditions that are optimal for meeting your goal.

I first learned about precommitment in the context of studying problem gambling. It is the idea that gamblers can mitigate potential losses by taking only a certain amount of cash to the casino. They don't take credit cards or a mobile phone that might allow them to somehow dial up for more funds. They take their car keys, they drive to a casino farther away from home than they'd prefer, and they take the amount of cash they're comfortable losing, and that's it. While this doesn't altogether eliminate the possibility of accessing more money, it does mean having to leave the casino, travel home (farther than you'd like), possibly go to a bank, return to the casino, and so forth. In other words, it attaches the barriers of time and effort to a likely bad decision. It reduces the possibility of a hasty, reactive choice and forces a more deliberate thought process where consequences are weighed. As humans, we are evolutionarily wired to take the least energy-expensive path. And oftentimes, heightened inconvenience is enough to short-circuit a bad decision.

In my own experience, the approach of precommitment was critical and may have saved me from myself. I realized early on that my inherent laziness and an insatiable appetite for junk food were incompatible with NBA stardom. But I knew that, with planning and structure, I could do something about it. Some people are able to casually integrate exercise into their day. Others, like me, will find every reason to avoid it unless it is scheduled into a precise time slot in our diary. So I created an iron-clad and inflexible workout schedule in order to ensure that exercise got done. Structure became a powerful tool and necessary for a boy who lacked the motivation and discipline to just "fit it in."

I needed an equally rigid structure around my diet, and this remains true even today. Like the gambler who leaves his bank card at home, I refrain from keeping any high-calorie treats in my kitchen or indeed in my house. If I want a doughnut (and I almost always do), I have to leave the house to get it or order it in, and by the time I consider either process, my mind has moved on. So, in that regard, my laziness works to my advantage.

In my NBA career, I managed to maintain 4 percent body fat, helped of course by the calories burned daily during practice and games. But I also relied upon precommitment, creating a structured and predictable environment that prevented me from sabotaging myself. Variety itself was a temptation—the craving for new and different flavors and the world of delicious possibilities offered on the grocer's shelves or a restaurant's menu. So, as an unsigned and undrafted rookie trying to secure a roster spot on the Cleveland Cavaliers, I decided not to engage with variety at all. I started eating the same meal every day for breakfast: steel-cut oatmeal with a teaspoon of honey and, separately, a tablespoon of natural peanut butter. And for lunch, broiled chicken breast with brown rice and broccoli. Every single day. For the entire basketball season. And for the 10 years that followed. Oatmeal in the morning. Broiled chicken in the day.

It was maddeningly boring. There were days that I was filled with rage staring at my plate. But it made me cherish dinner in a way that I never had before. And, crucially, it removed obstacles that threatened my ability to reach the performance level needed to compete in the NBA.

It is not a complex technique, precommitment. But it requires deep and objective self-assessment and accurate personal insights in order to apply it to best effect. So, again, I encourage you to stop for a moment and select one thing to start doing differently. But you should also take time to consider how you'll adjust your life to accommodate that change. If you are going to address the overly critical self-talk in your head, don't just commit to trying the Effective Feedback Model. Print out the questions and display them in a prominent spot in your workspace. If you are going to be a better meeting leader and attendee, how could you do that? Could you manage your calendar availability to limit back-to-back bookings? And block in a little advance time to actually think not only about the agenda and your personal stake but also about who the other attendees will be and how you can empower them to share their concerns, ideas, and voices. Maybe your one thing is just committing to getting better sleep. But what lifestyle change would be required to develop that skill? What marginal gain would be made simply by investing in a cheap digital alarm clock and leaving your phone on the charger in the kitchen?

Do one thing different for yourself for the benefit of everyone else. Develop one new habit. Make one change now, even if it's a "small" one. Because you do not do "small" anymore, remember. You are a giant now. Time to start acting like one.

Activity: The Wellbeing Tracker

At the end of every other day, perhaps at a specific time before sleep, rate your last couple of days on the seven areas for wellbeing included in the Wellbeing Tracker on the following page. In the first box, write a Y for "yes" or a N for "no" in terms of achieving any significant activity in that dimension on that day.

In the larger box to the right, jot a couple of words that indicate what you were able to do for a "yes," – something like – "60m Yoga class; friend nagged me" and for a "no," write what got in the way of doing enough of some activity to count as a "yes."

Keep track of your week for a month and then look back at any patterns you start to see. You can use different color highlighters to show your "yes" versus "no" days more clearly and dig into both to discover any themes that might help you get more Y in your week!

I Promise to Tend to Mind and Body

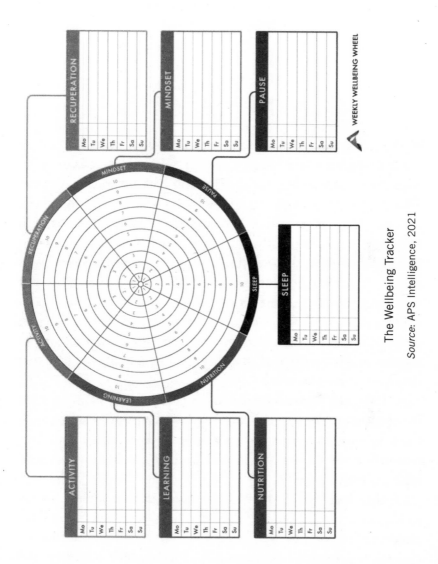

The Wellbeing Tracker

Source: APS Intelligence, 2021

CHAPTER 7

I Promise to Reflect Your Potential

To this point, our promises have been directed inward, focused on our relationships with ourselves—our self-awareness, our spirit of healthy competition, our courage and humility, our biases, our tolerance for discomfort, and, as a whole, our bodies and our minds.

These next few promises, in contrast, are made individually to the people who surround you and the people you impact directly. For many readers, this will include "direct reports," as well as employees farther down the traditional chain of command. But true giants do not require titles or labels or formal positions of authority over others. Given the proper support, they can assert power and make an impression from anywhere within the organization, simply by the way that they treat people. By the way that they look at people, even.

In 1902, the American sociologist Charles Cooley introduced the concept of "the looking-glass self," which posits that our identity is influenced and, in part, made up by how we see ourselves reflected in the faces of the people around us—how we imagine others perceive us to be.

Identity does not just percolate inside out—bubbling to the surface as a finished product. Rather, our identity—or at least our understanding of how we are supposed to feel about our identity characteristics—is a reflection of how we register, interpret, and process the reactions of those around us to us. Consider the influence that gives you: the power, at least in part, to determine how people feel about who *they* are.

If you're not vigilant, you can be an exaggerated funhouse mirror for everyone you come into contact with, reflecting back an unrecognizable and unwelcome reflection. The way you interact with people is critical. It can damage their self-regard and negatively impact their performance in ways you may never have intended. Or it can instill heightened and previously unreached levels of confidence. As a leader, a colleague and a giant, you must promise to reflect as accurately as possible the capabilities and promise of others; what others need to see in order to perform at the highest level—because that reflection has the power to tap into dormant reserves of unexplored potential.

As a boy, I believed myself to be beautiful and intelligent and special. Until I didn't. What changed? Nothing really, aside from the reflections around me. Throughout my early childhood, the primary reflection I saw was my mother's warm gaze, a constant and assuring presence.

I remember being on holiday with Mum and my sisters, the four of us packed into a rented caravan. There were stormy days that kept us trapped inside, with the deafening noise of rain pounding down on the tin roof. I loved being sequestered together during those times, cramped into our corners, each of us engrossed in our books. We were all avid readers. My mother had a thing for awful historical romance stories. And I would be immersed in science fiction, not yet seven but already well versed in Isaac Asimov—an intellectual beyond my years. That was how I saw it, at least, and in large part because that's how I saw my mother seeing it. I would catch her looking at me with an adoration and pride that let me know exactly who I was. I was smart. I was her clever boy. I knew in those moments, as I knew whenever I was in her presence, that I was capable of amazing things.

This sense of pride and self-assuredness lasted until I was about 11 when I advanced to secondary school. It was a school outside of the area around my family home, with an entirely new set of classmates and teachers who looked at me entirely differently than my mother did. There were three common reactions that my appearance evoked, and sadly these three reactions have grown no less common with age.

The first, then and now, was abject terror. People were terrified of me. I was unusually large, yes, but all the same I was a child, dressed in a ridiculous school uniform adorned with a gold braid and nervously clutching a bus pass and a briefcase (the only student in my class to have such a thing) and wearing unflattering National Health Service glasses. I was hardly a threat.

My wardrobe didn't seem to alter matters, though, and this also remains true today. Large and Black, I am the personification of what frightens people. Even in a three-piece suit, I can arouse palpable fear in others just by standing in line at an ATM.

The second reaction was mockery, though usually not to my face. I would walk by classmates and hear them laugh hysterically once I passed. It was beyond my comprehension. I had no responsibility for my height, and yet it caused me to be the butt of unremitting ridicule. I have grown accustomed to gawking stares now. I've come to expect that strangers will point me out to their friends and even try to discretely stand next to me for a stealth photo—a lasting memory of the time there was a carnival freak in their midst. (And yes, I can tell the difference on those rare occasions that an NBA fan approaches me—those tend to be far more polite interactions.)

The third reaction was the most perplexing and devastating for a boy who so valued being studious. In my new school, I found that people talked to me very slowly, as if I was fresh off the boat from a foreign, remote land. My appearance somehow communicated stupidity. Early in that first day at my new school, the students were brought together for an assembly. And as we were taking our seats, the first interaction I had was with a man, apparently the rugby coach, who enthusiastically said to me, "Of course you'll be playing rugby!"

No, no, no, I thought. You don't know me at all. Extreme cold, frozen pitches, sweating, being the biggest target on the field, no, no, no.

"No, thank you," I said with my brightest smile.

I knew even then I needed to avoid activities that could lead to brain injuries.

The coach stopped in his tracks with an expression of bemusement, as if to say "Get a load o' this guy," and then said more or less the same thing, in a stage-whispered comment to a few older kids who had witnessed the exchange.

"If he's not going to play rugby, what use is he?"

They all had a laugh.

I read Asimov when I was seven! You all misunderstand, I'm a clever boy!

No one looked at me like a clever boy on my first day. And for weeks, in my classes, in the halls, and on the bus, the faces reflecting back at me suggested strongly that I was a scary, primitive freak. I began to suspect my mother had deceived me. The story told by the way she looked at me was wildly at odds with what I was experiencing on a daily basis.

About a month into the school year, the teacher distributed a new book to the class. I had never heard the story before but was immediately captivated by its familiarity. We had time for reading during class, and when the lesson ended I hid the book under my desk and kept reading in secret. I read through lunch, I read on the bus, and I kept reading back at the house, waiting on the stairs inside for my mother to return home from work. She always carried a big set of keys so you could hear her coming from a mile away. And by the time she jangled those keys in the door, I was waiting for her—again, always with a flair for the dramatic—and I held the book out to her in my outstretched hand as if I'd just discovered a key piece of evidence in a longstanding mystery.

I had only one question after finishing the book.

"Mum ... Am I a *monster*?"

The book I had been reading all day was Victor Hugo's *The Hunchback of Notre-Dame*.

I knew I wasn't a literal hunchback, but I also knew all too well the travails of being treated as less than human. My peers were horrified by me and yet unafraid to insult and mock me as if poking a dangerous animal that they knew would not strike back. Like the citizens who scorned Quasimodo, they seemed to view me as intellectually stunted and emotionally illiterate. I saw it in their faces every day.

"You're not a monster, of course you're not," my mother assured me. "You're beautiful."

Her words were spoken with sincerity and love, and yet I was entirely unconvinced. For the first time in my life, I had the feeling that my mother was capable of lying to me. This realization, prompted by the tale of the hunchback, marked a clear turning point in my childhood. As unfortunate as my new reality was, things suddenly made a bit more sense—the way people outside of my family reacted to me. I was a monster, and that was that. So I started walking taller, with my head held high. Not because I was proud. On the contrary, I was just acclimating to the situation. My entire adolescence, I walked tall, always looking above and past the crowd. It was my way of tuning out a world that did not seem to have room for me. I could just look beyond it all, pixelating everyone below my sightline so they were only a blurred background.

It was a lonely existence, but it was necessary. I avoided crowds and public spaces as much as possible. Whenever I walked to a destination—school, the library, the bus stop—I walked with speed and purpose. I pixelated even people who might have enriched my life, people who might have genuinely cared for me and connected with me. I just couldn't take the chance. I couldn't risk hearing another degrading joke or seeing another aghast expression.

This is what happens as a result of exclusion. It is what happens when you don't see what you need to see reflected by those around you. It changes the way you interact with the world. You miss out on possible allies. You withdraw and retreat.

As giants and leaders, we have a responsibility to make sure that this never happens on our watch. And, again, this is not because it's important to be "nice." It is because, when we allow people to be seen as "less than" in any way, it limits their contributions. The mere feeling of being perceived as less valuable diminishes the value that a person can add to your organization.

The effect of expectations was well illustrated through a series of studies by the German-born American psychologist Robert Rosenthal. Most famously, in the 1960s, Rosenthal collaborated with the principal of a California elementary school, Lenore Jacobson, to examine whether teachers' expectations of students could impact performance—with those expectations thus serving as self-fulfilling prophecies of sorts. The experiment was conducted in each of the 18 classrooms in Jacobson's school. There were three classes in each grade (first through sixth, 6 through 11 years old), with students in each grade placed into classes of either above-average ability, average ability, or below-average ability.

At the beginning of the school year, students were given a nonverbal test of intelligence to establish a baseline for later reference. Their teachers were led to believe that the test results could identify intellectual "bloomers"—students who were primed to make surprising gains during the new school year. Although they didn't receive the actual test scores, each teacher was given the names of their supposedly blooming students, who made up roughly 20 percent of their classroom. In truth, the names had been chosen at random, and there was no actual linkage between the test results and intellectual blooming.

Eight months later, at the end of the school year, students were again administered the same test. In each grade, and especially in first and second, the students whom teachers had recognized as bloomers improved their scores by a margin that was greater than that of their control group classmates. This suggested that, when an elementary school teacher believes a student to have boundless potential, that perception, in a subtle but positive way, has an effect on the way the student performs. And, conversely, if the teacher has information (even erroneous information) indicating a student's potential is limited, that can negatively affect the child's educational outputs and outcomes.

Interestingly, in similar studies performed earlier in the context of a lab, Rosenthal referred to this effect as "unconscious experimenter bias." Over time, he dismissed the idea of "unconscious" and began referring to the phenomenon instead as the "unintentional interpersonal expectancy effect" or, in short, the Pygmalion effect, named after the mythological sculptor who fell in love with a statue he carved. The Pygmalion studies advanced the debate of whether expectations—well informed or otherwise—could create self-fulfilling prophecies and help certain students to thrive, potentially at the expense of students with lower expectations.

But the findings provided additional insight beyond the students' intellectual development. When asked at the end of the school year to describe their students' classroom behavior, teachers consistently spoke more favorably of the supposed bloomers. Those students were deemed to be more interesting, curious, and happy, and were given better chances to have long-term success. Such positive assessments could have been shaped by the intellectual development that played out during the course of the year. But there were students outside of the experimental group who also made notable intellectual gains, as measured by the increase in their test scores. Those students were not generally described with such affection, however. In fact, students from the non-bloomer control group who made the most dramatic test score improvements were often described by teachers as less well-adjusted and more likely to demonstrate undesirable behavior.

There are not many variables to explain the different outcomes for the two groups of students. They were randomly selected from pools of peers with similar skills, and teachers spent the same amount of time with students from both groups. The key difference was simply the teachers' expectations and the way those expectations were reflected back to students. What did it look like when a student from the control group got a C on a test versus when a supposed bloomer got a C? What subtle messages might a teacher have sent unwittingly when returning an A-grade paper to a bloomer and then returning an A-grade paper to an "ordinary" student?

The difference in the performance of bloomers was explained primarily by the faces of their teachers—faces that, with every interaction, reflected the message: "You are going to win." This is the message you should be sending to everyone around you, and especially to those who depend upon your leadership:

"I promise to look at you like I have faith in you. I promise to reflect back what you need to succeed."

This is not about lying to people—telling those who are not working hard that they are, pretending that those who have not delivered at the required level somehow have. Rather, this is about not clouding our judgments and infecting other people's sense of self with our doubts based on our so often flawed interpretations.

Delivering on this promise is even more important when your expression is directed toward members of minority communities. They've often spent a lifetime being looked at in less pleasant ways. They've become used to perceiving low expectations, suspicions, or worse in the eyes of others. And again, where traditional leadership roles are concerned, "minority" is not just about being non-white, non-male or non-heterosexual. It's about personality types and cognitive styles, neuro-atypicality, nationality and immigration status, and more.

Introverts need your nonverbal affirmation. People with disabilities need it. They need to understand that you believe they can reach their goals. Because they may not see that belief in others, and they may not see in your organization people like them who model the success they would like to achieve. More broadly, they have likely spent a lifetime informed by the reflections of popular culture, which only recently has begun to stretch the limits of what people like them can be. If you are an introvert or trans or dark-skinned or physically impaired, you may have never seen a path for where you want to go. Our job as giants is to engage with these and all people in a way that says: *Not only does your path to success exist, but I am going to walk it with you.*

This is why representation matters, both in the workplace and in culture. I will never forget the first time I saw the "Coming Soon" poster for *Black Panther* in a cinema lobby. I grew up a devotee of the comic series and had waited 40 years for that film. The image of T'Challa on his throne was my iPhone wallpaper for years. And while my friends were off at the loo, I remember standing in front of that poster in the lobby, captivated. Enamored. It was beautiful.

I was mesmerized by the collective imagery: the protagonist surrounded by his family and advisors and the enemies scheming his demise. It's a familiar film construct, but it struck me as completely new in this context. Thinking about *Black Panther* even today fills me with a pure joy that is polluted only by the fear that I'll never fully realize my inner T'Challa. T'Challa is the reflection that I both want and need to see in myself. He is Black in a world where Black is regal, Black is powerful, Black is intelligent, and Black is diplomatic. Black is complex and three-dimensional, with an arc that doesn't circle around constant tragedy or a struggle to define one's humanity.

T'Challa code-switches from moment to moment. He is both King of Wakanda and Black Panther, diplomat and defender, monarch and global superhero. And in whatever continent, costume, or context he finds himself, he is authentic to his core and he is respected. I feel this way sometimes—on the good days, when it is being reflected back at me. I am rarely as graceful or glamorous as a Chadwick Boseman, but there are days when I crush everything on my task list and dazzle my clients and uplift my team, and everyone looks at me like I'm an actual superhero. It fuels me, it feels wonderful! I float on those days!

But they can go sideways quickly. Just a couple weeks before seeing that poster, I'd been in the midst of one such day. I was scheduled to meet with a client, the global head of a professional services business that we've worked with for several years. I arrived at their office early, and rather than wait in the swanky top-floor meeting suite, I decided to stretch my legs and explore a bit. I had barely made it halfway down the hall when I was stopped by an employee, who literally grabbed my arm as I passed a break room and looked at me like his beloved pet was trapped under the refrigerator and it was my fault.

"Hello!?!" he said. "There's no bloody sparkling water in here!" He didn't let go.

You may find this incident hard to believe, particularly if you are not from a minority community. How could a five-foot-five man be so brazen and obnoxious as to grab a six-foot-nine stranger on the arm in a workplace, as if manhandling a misbehaving child? I have one answer to this, which is to say "Privilege," and to remind you that these types of microaggressions aren't as rare as perhaps you think.

But you might also wonder why I didn't react by ripping my arm from his grip or forcefully letting him know who I was and why I was there. You might wonder why instead I smiled and apologized even, saying, "I'm sorry. I'll get someone to sort that," before walking away to find a bathroom and splash cold water on my face. You might ask why I went one step farther along the way, and why, when passing a facility staff member, easily identified by a badge and uniform, I asked if he would look into the sparkling water deficit.

I did all of that—I turned the cheek, I shrunk on the spot—to protect myself. I knew that every visceral reaction that might feel better for me to act upon would only hurt me and my people—my team at APS as well as every Black person that this man would encounter in the future.

When I returned to the swish suite and was eventually joined by the big boss, he decided he wanted a different room. So we relocated, and as we walked to his preferred site, we passed the man who'd grabbed my arm. I nodded with as much dignity as I could muster and watched the penny drop and the color disappear from his face. Here was the monster, the token help provider of sparkling water, yukking it up with his boss as if we were lifelong friends. I'm sure he was terrified by his miscalculation, but that didn't provide solace or vindication. I had arrived at that meeting that day as a superhero, but, despite the success of my actual mission, I left my client's office feeling like the wounded monster of my childhood.

I thought about that man as well as the old rugby coach as I was staring in awe at T'Challa in the lobby. I thought about his exquisite nobility and the way he could strengthen his internal resolve through the slights and underestimations of the world. I could see my own face, 47 years old, in the reflection of that poster. And it was exactly what I've been looking for every day since I was a boy reading in the caravan—a superhero reflected back from the eyes of everyone around me. Some days I get that reflection—the best version of myself. Other days, it's Quasimodo.

Our job as giants is to make sure that people see us seeing them as superheroes and not as monsters. There is immeasurable power in your face alone! How do you receive someone who excitedly presents you with an idea that is only decent? Do you give it a cursory dismissal? Or do you highlight a morsel worth building upon or give some hope that, while this idea might not be ready for primetime, you remain a believer? What are the messages that you send without saying a word? What are the prophecies you encourage through unspoken expectations? The most impactful and memorable leaders make people feel good with just a look. Reflect the best in others, and that is what you are likely to get from them.

CHAPTER 8

I Promise to See You as an Individual and Not as a Job Description

Not long ago I spoke at a corporate leadership conference that was held on a cruise ship. The morning after my talk, quite early, there was a knock on my cabin door. I opened it, and there was a man, a steward, holding a platter with tea on it. He was offering it apparently as a gesture of kindness, having heard me reference tea, as well as the fact that I'm an early riser, repeatedly in my speech the previous day. What I hadn't mentioned in the speech was that I can also be a bit of a grouch first thing in the morning. So my initial reaction was a vacant and confused look, I'm sure. That reaction we occasionally have as leaders when one of our people does something they believe to be profound. And we look at them thinking, *Err ... OK. Thanks?*

So I thanked him and was trying to get him to hand over the tea so I could close the door. But he looked past me into the room, where I had the TV on, which to my embarrassment was playing the speech I'd given the day before. I hastily tried to explain that I don't usually wake up at 6:30 to watch myself on TV but I'd fallen asleep with it on the night before, watching a replay of the other keynote talk by Mary Portas.

And he nodded and said, "Yes, we get these programs on the TVs in our cabins, too."

His "we" was carrying a lot of weight. There was a hint of resignation to it, as if he was referring to himself not as an individual but as an anonymous representative of an invisible underclass.

But, on the flip side, it revealed a selflessness; he was visiting as a delegate, with the interests of sharing some collective insight, in mind.

"We saw your speech on the TV in our cabins and we knew you'd see us," he said, gesturing toward the TV.

I tried not to let it show, but I felt terrible upon hearing this because the entire time we'd been standing there, I'd been imagining grabbing the tea, slamming the door, and returning to bed. Instead, I opened it and invited him in. He sat on a chair, and I poured us each a cup and sat across from him on the bed, and we drank the tea in silence. I learned about the power of silence during my time training to be a marriage and family therapist. In today's utilization culture, we don't appreciate silence as we should. Breakthroughs and even innovation can often come from people sitting together quietly until they have something important to share.

Eventually, the steward looked at me and started to speak, almost in a whisper.

"We're invisible on this boat. When passengers go by, we press ourselves into the wall so we don't get in the way. When our managers go by, we press ourselves into the wall so they don't think we're doing something wrong.

"They treat us like vending machines," he said. "They flip their instructions at us like a coin and then wait, tapping their foot, until we give them exactly what they want. The most human inter-action we have on this boat is when someone flips their instruction at us and we can't give them what they want. And then it's like they want to shake us, like whatever they want is *stuck* inside us."

He went on to describe the dynamics and politics of life and work on the boat in a way that reflected a complex and nuanced understanding of how his organization worked. He spoke elegantly but with a simplicity that allowed me—a complete outsider who knows nothing about the cruise industry—to get a full picture of what he and his colleagues and supervisors and passengers experience every day. And I sat listening to all of this, quite astounded.

In the little "free" time he had, this young man and others like him, took the time to listen to the conference speeches. And in mine he heard an opportunity. With that opportunity, he did something bold and more than a little vulnerable—never mind demonstrating some creativity—in showing up with the tea—a brilliant anticipation of needs—to get in the door. He took a chance to approach someone who I think he imagined might possess words of guidance that would help improve the collective experience of him and his fellow stewards. And he did so at great risk to himself; as he noted, his supervisors would certainly not have approved of this uninvited visit.

What he did was leadership, all of it.

Through just this brief conversation, it was obvious that the steward was capable of so much more than what his primary responsibilities demanded and limited him to. But such cases are more common than they should be. Organizations bemoan the time and resources that must be spent recruiting "talent"—*there's a "war for talent" going on out there*! But oftentimes talent is right under our noses, but not in the right roles. And this is because the "talent," or "human resources," is not viewed as human. Workers have been largely commoditized, and, as such, they are separated and crammed into labeled boxes and confined lines of progression, from which escape is rare. Once you've brought the tea, you can't be an administrator. Once you've been an administrator, you can't be a salesperson. Once you've been a salesperson, you can't be a techie.

My team and I work with global organizations of immense complexity, with all the challenges of operating across jurisdictions and various regulatory alignments, and with huge numbers of people. I know it can be hard to see a worker as a person through all that bureaucracy, but organizations that will thrive in the future will flow with the recent humanization of the workforce through and post the COVID crisis and will embrace the need for talent to move and roles to evolve in a way they never have before. This rethink is illustrated by a recent McKinsey study in which the authors concluded that, between 2016 and 2030, between 75 and 375 million workers globally will need to move out of their occupational category to find work.[1]

The old, rigid, and sometimes unspoken boundaries on what people can contribute are antithetical to the ideals of innovation and disruptive thinking. They diminish performance, and they make people miserable. A lose–lose. Nearly every organization I work with is striving toward some form of automation or development in artificial intelligence that will make their processes and technology more human-like. And, in the meantime, many of those same organizations are unwittingly making their people feel more and more like robots. Like vending machines. Like that young steward from the ship.

And the problem with vending machines is they don't innovate well; they don't adapt. You put in a certain amount of money and make your selection, and the machine grants you that selection. If you ask for a chocolate bar, it gives you a chocolate bar. It isn't permissioned to assess your selection and recommend a better alternative in your interest. It can't offer you a carrot or a side of crisps. If it gets stuck and fails to deliver, it can't do anything but wait to be shaken. If it accidentally delivers two bars, it can't retrieve one.

We can expect vending machine service if we treat our people like vending machines, and that will be OK some of the time. But winning in the long term and through inevitable bouts of volatility requires more than vending machine service. So that is why giants promise to see and treat people as unique, individual beings and as more than just their job descriptions.

The commoditization of people in the workplace is nothing new. In fact, it's embedded into the language we use to refer to our people, be they "employees," "talent," or "human resources." These terms strip away a layer of humanity, imposing uniformity in its place. They discourage nuance in favor of categories. They sound at home in organizations that fail to recognize or appreciate the unique and important abilities that every person, if they feel engaged and included, brings to the table.

But the dehumanizing effect of nomenclature is mild when compared to the damage done by onerous processes and policies, from ineffective performance review routines to inefficient legacy practices to inflexible utilization targets. These contribute to an environment that systematically dehumanizes our colleagues. And once you start turning people into machines, commodities, or "resources," you can do unconscionable things to them. Because the moment that someone is less than human—even by a fraction—what we consider reasonable in their treatment changes radically, and not for the better. At its most violent and wicked extremes, we have seen where this leads; discrimination, slavery, and genocide have invariably targeted groups who were first framed as somehow less than human.

But we have also seen the extremes of what commoditizing and dehumanizing people can lead to in the workplace. These examples may not be as bloody or violent, but they are certainly cause for concern, if not alarm. One high-profile incident was the forcible removal of a United Airlines passenger from an overbooked flight in 2017. The passenger, David Dao Duy Anh, had already boarded the sold-out flight and was one of four travelers who were randomly selected for involuntary removal to make room for airline employees who needed to get to the destination airport. When Dao, a fully paid customer, declined to be bumped, the crew summoned airport security, who quite literally pulled him out of his seat and dragged him down the aisle against his will, to the horror and bewilderment of fellow passengers documenting the scene with cell phone cameras. As the footage went viral in the days that followed, United CEO Oscar Munoz compounded the damage by defending the removal as "re-accommodating the customers." Also in the days that followed, Munoz lost a planned promotion to Chairman of the Board, United became a laughing stock, and its market value dropped by 4 percent, roughly 770 million dollars. Why?

It is perhaps little surprise that the airline industry would produce such a textbook example of what can happen when organizations stop viewing people as people. So many aspects of being a passenger have been dehumanized through the years. So the United incident, while outrageous, is also a natural and even predictable outcome of a culture gone wrong. If you generally treat your customers like excess baggage, you would, of course, think it's OK to drag them down the aisle like excess baggage, should they present a logistical inconvenience. When organizations treat people—both their workforce and their customers—as robots or cattle or vending machines, it becomes acceptable to demand compliance to even the most egregious of orders and policies. And an acquiescent, beaten-down rank and file will follow orders, tuning out their own logic, ethics, morality, and judgment. In the service of their employer, they will treat a paying customer less well than excess baggage despite the existential threat to their employer's reputation and value.

This is why we cannot lose sight of humanity and individualism. And why we must promise to see more in our people than just what is outlined in their job descriptions. Organizational culture depends upon it. Realizing the full potential of our people depends upon it. And, ultimately, winning depends upon it.

But there are factors that work against us and make it difficult to fulfil this promise. I have already mentioned the stultifying effect of bureaucratic processes and policies that numb the mind and are often unnecessary. Further, though, as we become more skilled in the technical demands of our work and more familiar with the routines of our workplaces, there is a natural tendency toward desensitization. It becomes easier to put on blinders and operate on autopilot when carrying out responsibilities that have become habitual. Add to this toxic stew the cult of busy, which mandates that all serious professionals look and sound like they have no time to breathe, and you have a recipe for disaster.

Again, it is fascinating to watch this ironic evolution in the modern working world—the development of artificial intelligence and the creation of generic, almost cookie-cutter-like workforces. We are mining data at an unprecedented rate and creating ever smarter algorithms in an effort to mimic human intelligence. And meanwhile we are operating with policies, procedures, language, an approach to people, and fixed mindsets around inclusion and human capability that transform people into predictable, indistinguishable, and ultimately disposable automatons. We are living in a time in which our brightest minds are trying to create human-like machines while making people themselves more machine-like. But wait—it gets worse!

Traditionally, most corporate entities—not all, but most—have been triangular in structure and hierarchy. At the top, you have a small group of "elite" leaders, who generally make the most money while arguably contributing the least. At the bottom, you have that indispensable bedrock of the rank and file who are keeping the wheels turning. That's where the grunts are doing the real dirty work and, in doing so, mastering skills and developing critical competencies. And, ideally, the best and brightest from that group will ascend into that center layer of the triangle that we sometimes refer to dismissively as "middle management." These are the people charged with ensuring that work gets done, top-tier managers are kept happy, and the rank and file are kept reasonably satisfied.

But what we are seeing in many organizations is a change in the shape of its workforce. What once was a triangle (▲) is now something of a flat-bottomed rhombus (◆). The modern world has nibbled away at the base; information processing and basic tasks no longer require contributions from members of the bottom layer. Robotics, artificial intelligence, automation, offshoring, descriptive and predictive analytics—they've all taken a bite and, as a result, fewer actual humans are needed in that bottom layer.

That creates an interesting problem for the middle layer. Because when you had a larger base, you had a vast pool of people developing skills that would make them attractive candidates for the middle layer. You could afford for some natural attrition and still be left with a strong selection of experienced talent to ascend into management roles. But now that pool is getting smaller, and there's less room for attrition. It becomes more challenging to find people who are truly prepared for the middle-layer jobs. People who have had time to not only master basic tasks and skills but also develop intellectual and emotional intelligence around their workplace and industry.

The unfortunate end result is that more workers are ascending to the middle layer without the skills or training necessary to deal with, let alone lead, other human beings. First-time managers are being elevated to that role with undeveloped competencies around motivating, empathizing with, and collaborating with people—identifying and extracting the best from them. Collectively, "middle management" is getting even worse in such areas, and it hasn't been very good, to begin with!

It is past time that we reverse this trend toward the dehumanization of our workforce and start tapping into the unique talent that is right under our noses. To do this—to recognize the potential that lurks beyond job description—requires that we see every person as an individual and act in ways that are tailored to their individual needs. It requires that we take the emotional labor of work every bit as seriously as the technical labor.

Technical labor is usually predictable and well defined and the focus of our daily efforts. It encompasses the nuts and bolts of what it takes to "get the job done." Basic skills, knowledge, and cognitive capabilities can be acquired through technical labor alone, as well as a fundamental awareness around processes and procedures, business strategy, and human resource management.

But emotional labor is the domain in which leaders distinguish themselves, for better or worse. Emotional labor encompasses self-awareness, personal vigilance, emotional intelligence, and intellectual curiosity about other people and the way they work. Making the effort to see people as individuals and helping them recognize and realize their potential beyond job description is an investment of emotional labor.

The advent of COVID and its spread across the world forced companies into acknowledging the holistic nature of their people—for some this was the first time. Organizations had to account for families sharing a computer for video conferencing, they saw employees' most intimate spaces and day-to-day watched on as isolation, crowded circumstances, lack of exercise and sleep, and all the other horrors of lockdown laid siege to their mental health. They saw their people *as* people and once seen, there is no going back to pretending that they can only be understood as units of productivity.

The concept of emotional labor was introduced in 1983 by the American sociologist Arlie Russell Hochschild. She described it as the way we manage and manifest emotion in the workplace in order to meet the requirements of our jobs. The more obvious examples of this come from the service industry, where face-to-face customer engagement demands that workers create and maintain a positive experience through regulation and presentation of emotion. But Hochschild also noted the importance of emotional labor in workplaces that "allow the employer, through training and supervision, to exercise a degree of control over the emotional activities of employees."

Hochschild noted that emotional labor in the workplace has traditionally been expected from women more than men—the idea being that emotional moderation of any environment is a woman's burden. It is a ridiculous notion but one that has proven durable. Recall the word association experiment discussed in Chapter 4 and the descriptors that people used to capture their views of women in the workplace—words around nurturing and caring and mothering.

Creating an emotional environment where people can thrive is everyone's responsibility and particularly that of leaders, because we need our people to deliver consistently and at high levels. So what could be more important than allowing people to focus exclusively on external battles against competitors, disruptive agents, marketplace threats, and sociopolitical change? You can either have them focused on that, or you can have them constantly ruminating and worrying, churning and burning energy, worried about the last interaction with their colleague or manager.

Emotional labor means taking the time to understand individuals' emotional needs. And that is serious, selfless work. It's not as simple as the Golden Rule implies. That rule is more of a narcissist's charter than good advice: *Do unto others as you would have them do unto you.* No. Why would anyone in this increasingly diverse, international, and connected world, imagine that how they want to be treated is a good template for the rest of the world?!

How about: Do unto others as *they* would have done to *them*? When it comes to doing unto others, there is no one-size-fits-all way. And if there was, it would not be to think of how *you* would want it done. Emotional labor is figuring out the different ways that different people might respond to words and actions, even when they are the exact same words and actions! Every interaction is like the giant's handshake; it needs to be customized and tailored to the individual needs of the other party.

Imagine a client dinner scenario with a few parties from each side. One of the clients mentions that she's been taking painting classes, or even that she knows someone who's taking painting classes, and because you're collegial within your collegial office, you happen to know that one of your dinner colleagues also does some painting. You've even heard she's quite good! You could mention this at the table, and your artist colleague might appreciate the opportunity to speak to her craft. Or you could mention it and your artist colleague might feel embarrassed and exposed. Knowing a couple of things about people—that they "like painting"—doesn't tell you much.

We will cover feedback in the next promise, but it is an area where a tailored approach is clearly needed. There are some people who respond optimally if you note publicly that they can do better. You can look at them in a full meeting room and say, "Come on, now. You didn't do X, Y, and Z in the last quarter, and I know you can do better and we need you to do better." Some people could be motivated by this; being held accountable before their colleagues fires them up in a positive way. But others would be mortified and demoralized. They may be better motivated by receiving the feedback during a post-meeting chat where there is more one-on-one time and fewer witnesses. The approaches differ, but the end goal is the same: how can I engage you, specifically, in a way that gets the best result from you, specifically?

When you invest emotional labor and start viewing and treating people as individuals, it unleashes their potential to contribute more than you thought possible when you hired them. More than you asked for in the job posting. It allows them to be a true team-mate. This is one key difference between teams and groups. In groups, your job description is the endpoint of responsibility. In teams, it is only the starting point.

I am reluctant to draw comparisons between the workplaces that most of you are familiar with and the workplace of sport and, specifically, the NBA, because, in most ways, they're radically different worlds—not so much apples and oranges, but vegetables and minerals. But there was one clear truth I learned in sport, during my first season with Orlando Magic, that, while absurd and completely unrelatable, is also a perfect illustration of extracting value for the greater good from what falls outside of individual job descriptions.

When I arrived in Orlando in 2003, I had already played a season with the Cleveland Cavaliers and a couple of seasons over-seas, so I was not a true "rookie." But in the Magic locker room, and, for the purposes of this story, in the Magic team plane, I was very much a rookie.

I was also a bit weird in their eyes. Part of this was simply being a foreigner at a time when teams were still less international than they are in today's NBA. But I was also studying for my doctorate in psychology, which was, at least for that peer group, an unusual side endeavor (though one that fits well with the NBA lifestyle, where you have a healthy income and abundant downtime for reading and studying).

We traveled in spacious 747s that carried about 20 passengers. And as was true of every team bus or plane that I ever traveled on, there was a clear hierarchy to the seating assignments. So, when we first started traveling in preseason, I knew not to sit at the sole four-top table because that's traditionally where the veterans sit to play cards or shoot the shit. However, after only a game or two, I boarded the plane and one of the vets who usually occupied the table suggested that I sit there instead. So I did. But no one joined me. I sat there alone.

After the plane took off and leveled, I opened my laptop and began to work, trying to act like there was nothing unusual about me sitting at the table, obsessing over whether everyone hated me or was conspiring against me in some elaborate prank that was sure to humiliate. Eventually, one of my teammates approached and asked if he could sit. "Meech," he said. "I've got a problem."

Before I even heard what the problem was, I knew that something important had happened. My peers had identified an additional value that I could add to the team. Outside of on-court communication, I'd only shared a few brief conversations with this person. But nonetheless he saw in me someone who could help him. I was not being ostracized. I was not being scorned. I was literally being put in a seat where I could offer something unique to my teammates far beyond what I was technically paid to do.

The teammate's problem, as it turned out, was that his wife didn't like his girlfriend very much. You can relate, right?

Perhaps not.

But we talked about this at 30,000 feet, and during the weeks and road trips that followed, more of my teammates started visiting the four-top to seek counsel on both the absurd and the mundane. They entrusted me to offer guidance in their relationships with coaches, fellow teammates, spouses, children, extended family, hangers-on, financial advisers, agents, and yes, the many girlfriends. And it was as if they had found an additional utility from me. There were certain statistical expectations for my output on the court. But, in only a couple months, my teammates discovered that the undrafted rookie off the scrap heap had an additional competency. Beyond points and rebounds, my postgraduate training in psychology could also be to their benefit.

This is how it works on high-performing teams, where the job description is only the start of what one is permitted to be. In my view, it is not a coincidence that the Magic team on which I felt most embraced and encouraged as a complete person was also the team on which I achieved the most professional success, individually and collectively.

It may be easier to work with machines, but the words that will define organizational success in the future are transformation, innovation, disruption, and resilience. These are human words, intrinsically tied to properties that only humans can manifest, at least for now. And organizations that are serious about winning appreciate that every moment an employee feels less human, they are less and less able, not to mention willing, to demonstrate those qualities that are so important.

When we ignore the unique complexities of the humans in our human resources and box them into their job descriptions, we create a grim existence where people are not quite full people. When we illuminate those complexities, we avail ourselves of an entirely new range of possibility. We create conditions in which the most unlikely of people, in the most improbable of circumstances, can become extraordinary.

The way we understand many role descriptions needs to shift. Whether it's social or a job description, people seem to imagine there is a tiny, barely capable version of a person stretching to occupy that cavernous role, when in reality the idea of a giant being suffocated by a label is probably a more apt metaphor.

CHAPTER 9

I Promise to Deliver Timely and Effective Feedback

There are legitimate reasons to avoid difficult conversations, particularly around feedback. Such dialogues are challenging and energy expensive. We don't know what to say, or we fear that we'll get it wrong. There's a chance our intentions will be misperceived and our subject will get upset and become emotional. And by talking about something, we may fear we'll make it worse and injure our relationship with the recipient. We imagine and fear a damaged future.

Biology gives us a natural excuse to cower from these conversations. The deterrents listed above ring alarm bells in the amygdala, the "emotional" or "irrational" part of our brain. And the response is an "amygdala hijack" of sorts, which sends us into a state of flight, fight, or freeze and makes it difficult for us to successfully address performance and behavior.

The good news is that delivering timely and effective feedback is just an ordinary skill. So, like any ordinary skill, it can be improved with practice and discipline. And as tricky conversations become more familiar, they will become less of a threat to your amygdala. They will become easier, and you will become better at them. Because what happens if you don't? What happens if you put off feedback or put forth only a half-hearted effort? The problems get worse, right? Your own situation gets worse. The situations of others get worse. And you end up needing to have a difficult conversation anyway, only now it's more difficult because now everything is worse.

We promise to deliver timely and effective feedback because our people deserve it and need it in order to thrive. When we avoid constructive criticism out of fear that it might come across as cruel, we do them a tremendous disservice. What could be crueler than knowingly letting a colleague repeat errors or act in counterproductive ways, oblivious to their missteps?

You may recall seeing footage of President Trump ascending the stairs of Air Force One with a trail of toilet paper stuck to the bottom of his shoe. It was a viral moment that provided some with a good laugh, but it was also an extremely informative moment. The most widely shared video was tightly focused on the president alone, the sad, sticky fragment of toilet paper dragging behind. But when you zoom out to a wider angle, you see a whole host of people bearing witness in silence. All told, at least a dozen people surround the president as he exits the armored "Beast" limousine and heads up the stairs—Secret Service officers, flight crew, White House staff. And no one says a word. Those who traveled with him in the car and those watching him walk, they all know quite well that this embarrassment will be broadcast across the globe.

What does this incident tell us? What does it mean when every single member of Trump's motorcade stays silent as he escorts this uninvited hitchhiker out of the Beast and up the stairs, with a fleet of cameras broadcasting to the world? We can't say for sure, but the options aren't great. Either they simply don't care enough about the man to bother helping him. Or they fear how he might react to their help. It's like being at a dinner party and noticing a chunk of greens lodged in the teeth of a guest. Your reaction to that situation says a lot about your feelings toward that person. If you respect, trust, and care for them, you will deliver some kind of feedback. Even if you have to create an excuse to have them leave the table with you to "help in the kitchen" or "share some important work news in private"—you find a way.

It's not a form of kindness to watch one of your colleagues go around doing stuff that is the equivalent of greens in the teeth or toilet paper on the shoe. And, conversely, when someone constructively points out your own greens-in-teeth or toilet paper, it should be welcomed as a gesture of trust and goodwill.

Again, delivering timely and effective feedback is a basic skill that is attainable to all. It requires practice, though, and repetition. And not many of us put in that work, partly because of the previously listed deterrents to giving feedback, but also because our employers don't explicitly demand it on an ongoing basis; thus it's easy to avoid. Perhaps there's an annual appraisal cycle with one or two additional check-ins during the year. But we all know how these work or, rather, don't work. They're usually based on a numeric ranking scheme—because what feels better than seeing a year of hard work reduced to a number between 1 and 5? Or, more realistically, a number between 2 and 4? You get a 4 if they really want you to stay (but don't want to pay you more); a 3 means average and a whole group of people are placed here on the basis of talent, personality, tenure, or a simple hesitance to have a substantive conversation with them, and a 2 if they are preparing you for bad news next cycle—or perhaps giving you a chance to improve. Too many 5s is inconvenient and expensive in a world where too many organizations think there can only be a finite number of high performers. And if performance does warrant a 1, the situation is probably already being addressed with the manager (making the demotivating 1 all the more gratuitous).

All of this is made even more irrelevant when you consider "fixed distributions," where the number of people who can be at each level is already preordained on a curve, and the criteria for measuring achievement are far from standardized and objective.

People are not numbers. And performance cannot be accurately measured by scores tallied on a card at the end of the year. This is especially so in cases where the person interpreting the card is not intimately familiar with the employee or is influenced by recency bias or their own perceptions of what outputs matter most. These formal appraisals are generally rubbish and poor vehicles for delivering feedback that inspires high performance.

Preparing and delivering effective, timely feedback is not something that is done for finite periods of time. It's something that you do constantly; it's ongoing. It's a never-ending series of "micro-appraisals." It's arriving at work every day with open eyes and a commitment to notice significant, even if small, behaviors and actions, and to document or follow up on them within 24 hours. Embracing this concept of micro-appraisals will contribute to an environment where feedback is the norm. They afford us more opportunities to get those reps and practice giving and receiving feedback. And if they are employed consistently, micro-appraisals will make those formal appraisals less daunting and more impactful.

This approach to feedback relies upon assertive observation of even the smallest events. It's not as simple as acknowledging and assessing what is obvious in front of you. It requires a constant state of high alert and proactive vigilance for identifying meaningful moments. Every meeting, project, client call, presentation, report, and email exchange must be seen as an opportunity to recognize notable behavior, whether notably good or notably poor.

When we do recognize these notable behaviors or interactions, timely follow-up is critical. What are the implications of what you have observed? And what do you do with those implications? Perhaps you've learned enough to offer immediate feedback, or perhaps you need to ask questions to learn more. Perhaps the incident provides a learning tool for the broader working group and can be used as such with the permission of those who were involved. Or perhaps your only action is to send yourself a one-sentence email about the incident, a reminder to follow up on the matter during a formal appraisal or a more appropriate moment.

To discern whether a piece of feedback is worthy of bringing to the fore, it is useful to revisit the questions from the Effective Feedback Model (EFM) (see Chapter 1). When we discussed those earlier, it was within the context of processing internal and external feedback. But if you ask yourself these questions before delivering feedback, it will clarify the meaning and value of the message you're about to send.

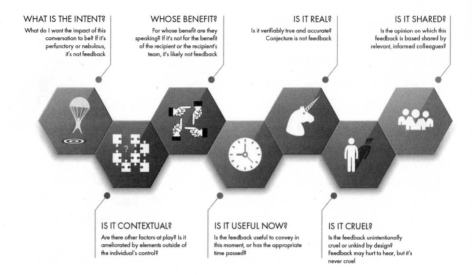

WHAT IS THE INTENT?
What do I want the impact of this conversation to be? If it's perfunctory or nebulous, it's not feedback

WHOSE BENEFIT?
For whose benefit are they speaking? If it's not for the benefit of the recipient or the recipient's team, it's likely not feedback

IS IT REAL?
Is it verifiably true and accurate? Conjecture is not feedback

IS IT SHARED?
Is the opinion on which this feedback is based shared by relevant, informed colleagues?

IS IT CONTEXTUAL?
Are there other factors at play? Is it ameliorated by elements outside of the individual's control?

IS IT USEFUL NOW?
Is the feedback useful to convey in this moment, or has the appropriate time passed?

IS IT CRUEL?
Is the feedback unintentionally cruel or unkind by design? Feedback may hurt to hear, but it's never cruel

The Effective Feedback Model

Source: APS Intelligence, 2021

The Effective Feedback Model

What is the feedback's intent?

When you schedule a meeting, setting clear objectives helps make the most of the time. The same is true of feedback. If you can clearly articulate the objective(s) of delivering a piece of feedback, it is more likely to be received as substantive feedback. What are the specific behaviors or actions that you are addressing? If your rationale for the feedback is muddled or imprecise—if you're trying to correct or highlight something that you cannot clearly explain yourself—then this is a sign that the line of feedback may be suspect and requires further thought.

Is the feedback contextual?

Have you done the due diligence of identifying any mitigating factors that may be influencing the behavior in question? This is just another reason why it is so important that we invest time in knowing our people. If we don't have a basic understanding of any personal or professional challenges they may be facing, we can't know how those challenges are impacting job performance or satisfaction.

Who is benefiting from the feedback?

There should be an obvious answer to this question. And if there's not, or worse, if it is the wrong answer, then the feedback is misguided and should be withheld. To avoid any doubt, feedback should benefit the organization, for sure, but in that moment of delivery, it must be given in a way that benefits the recipient. Character assassinations are not feedback, ad hominem attacks are not feedback, frustrated, emotional outbursts are not feedback—in part because the beneficiaries are not the recipient.

Accurately identifying the beneficiary requires that you be in a proper state of mind. Because in the heat of the moment, judgment is often clouded. And this can lead to delivering feedback in a way that achieves little more than satisfying the person giving the feedback.

This bears emphasis before moving to the next question. If you are stressed, it will be reflected in the delivery of your feedback. And the danger here is that your stress level and its effect on you may not even be apparent. Studies show that, as anxiety rises, our metacognition skills decline. Metacognition is the ability to think about and understand how you think—knowing your mental and emotional tendencies and how they affect decisions and perceptions. Researchers have found that, when you're not very stressed—a 2 out of 10 on the stress scale—you're likely to know that. By contrast, when you're a 9 out of 10 stressed, impaired metacognition might delude you to thinking you're only a 4 or 5. So vigilance is imperative here. Before delivering feedback, be sure that you can clearly state—with a sound mind—that the recipient is the primary beneficiary and that the feedback is in no way driven by your own needs or mental state.

Is the feedback useful *now*?

Remember, when a notable behavior is observed, there should be prompt follow-up. However, that immediate action will not necessarily be delivering feedback. There may be tense incidents that need time to cool down and topics better suited toward formal appraisal rather than quick, ongoing micro-appraisals. If the time is not right yet, though, don't let the moment pass altogether. That's where those self-addressed email reminders come in handy. Create a subfolder for each of your reports, where you collect notes for future reference. But don't wait too long! That's the flipside of the coin: feedback related to a specific observation loses impact with the passage of time. It's like rubbing a puppy's nose in a urine stain long after it's peed over the rug. There is a weakened association between the act and the consequence. So if you observe something that warrants intervention in the immediate term, it is imperative that you find the time to bring it forward before it's too late.

Is the feedback real?

This is a pretty simple one. Do you have an accurate and comprehensive understanding of the action or behavior that your feedback is targeting? Or have you made an assumption? Have you inferred intent? Have you given your subject an honest benefit of the doubt? Or are there still questions that have not been asked, which could alleviate uncertainty and suspicion. You may not be able to acquire enough information to have the full picture in advance, but feedback should avoid supposition and conjecture as much as possible.

Is the feedback cruel?

You are not obligated to give feedback in a way that feels good because critical feedback does not always feel good. Critical feedback can dent the armor of ego and diminish a sense of competence or autonomy. It can wound and hurt. But it should never be cruel; it should never be delivered with a sense of harm as the intent.

You can think of this as the difference between rugby and boxing. In rugby, you can definitely get a concussion. But the aim of rugby is not to deliver a brain injury. In boxing, you can get a concussion because the aim of boxing is to concuss. Boxing is a sport where brain injury—a knockout—is the goal.

There's a difference between tough, objective, critical feedback that may hurt but also informs and develops, and feedback that is given with the intent of leaving a scar or a permanent sense of shame and inadequacy with no care as to whether it will enable development and growth.

Is the feedback shared?

Would the feedback come as no surprise to others who are familiar with the recipient or the situation? Or are you alone in your assessment? An outside opinion can be a valuable sanity check when you're considering whether to give feedback. And if others are directly affected by the behaviors or actions in question, it may be advisable to consult them as well, if appropriate.

The idea of running every bit of potential feedback through seven questions might seem excessive. But, with repetition and practice, the exercise becomes routine. So commit the questions to memory, in order, and make a habit of asking each one to sort effective feedback from feedback that is underdeveloped or problematic. Before long, the questioning will become engrained and the model will feel second nature.

Of course, the Effective Feedback Model measures only the potential value of a given piece of feedback. How that feedback is transmitted is equally important. But here, too, an easy-to-remember and deliberate structure can guide the way. I refer to this as the Five Cs of Feedback: Curiosity, Courtesy, Clarity, Consequence, and Commitment. Focusing on these while crafting feedback helps to create conditions of engagement and lessens the chances that the recipient will become defensive.

- **Start with curiosity and with questions.** "I noticed this event occurred, can you tell me a little about it?" "How have you been feeling about this particular situation?" And when you ask a question, leave space for the answer. Take the time to understand the response that you're given, as curious in your listening as you are in your interrogation. This allows you to gather information, but it also acknowledges that you may not have all the facts. Creating a two-way conversation builds trust and makes it less likely that you'll be viewed as judgmental.

- **Secondly, and always, you must show courtesy.** Regardless of how you may feel about a given situation or person, you must always maintain the high ground and role-model the right way to handle problems. Thank the person for taking the time to sit with you. Make it clear that you appreciate the discussion may be awkward or uncomfortable. But never resort to sarcasm, passive aggression, put-downs, name-calling, or raising your voice. This will only obscure your message and put your audience on the defensive. Preserving a high level of civility and courtesy keeps your audience engaged and gives you the best chance of being heard.

- **Make sure there is clarity.** By processing your feedback through the Effective Feedback Model, you have hopefully gained a sense of clarity around it. But when nerves and heightened tension come into play, it is easy for that clarity to get lost. So avoid generalizations and hypotheticals and emphasize specifics. Anchor your feedback to actual events, and make sure that your focus is clearly on behaviors and actions rather than personalities.

  If we want to prevent people from repeating mistakes, we need to be specific about what is actually causing the problem. And this is true for positive feedback as well. The concentration of this chapter has been critical feedback, as that is generally more challenging. But positive feedback must also be specific in order to be effective. Generic praise is lazy and painfully transparent and can have the unintended effect of generating resentment. In both praise and criticism, be detailed and clear.

- **There also must be clarity around the consequence.** Illuminating poor behavior or performance is not enough if its impact is not discussed. Quite often, conversations get lost in the theoretical of what words or actions mean or what their intent is. If you can root the feedback instead in the impact and consequences of those words and actions, it becomes harder to refute. If an action is having a tangible impact on another person or on the business, there is a real and undeniable consequence and a reason to alter that behavior.

- **Lastly, elicit a commitment.** The entire point of sharing feedback is to encourage modification or reinforcement of behavior. So, when concluding these conversations, don't be afraid to ask for a commitment. Doing so clarifies future expectations and strengthens the recipient's sense of accountability to continued improvement. It marks a new beginning and hopefully a refreshed mutual understanding of the way forward.

Even highly skilled and veteran managers can be exhausted by appraisal and feedback discussions. But once you've wrapped one up, try not to hastily move to the next thing, eager to put the discussion behind you. Take a breath and try to spend a moment with the perspective of an objective viewer. What went well and what could have gone better? If you can identify that, you can repeat or improve upon it. You can start embedding habits and best practices. You can better anticipate the rough spots. And, in doing so, you will be more apt to get it right the next time around.

The promise to deliver timely and effective feedback is not one many of you will be eager to embrace. But, remember, it is simply a promise to consistently perform a basic action that is completely within your capabilities and requires only practice, practice, practice. The more you do it, the better you'll be and the easier it will get.

Feedback is the greatest gift you can give your colleagues. They are going to get greens stuck in their teeth and toilet paper stuck on their feet. But, when that happens, don't shrink from the moment. Love and respect them enough to let them know.

Activity: Assess Feedback Using the EFM

Spend some time reviewing the most recent feedback you've given and received. Filter it through the EFM and assess the quality and effectiveness of both the feedback you gave and the feedback you received.

Activity: Commit to Using Micro-Appraisal

With colleagues and direct reports, follow the steps outlined below. This doesn't just work with direct reports, but peers and managing up, too. There are plenty of people with partners who would also appreciate the specific things they do being noticed and remarked upon over the course of a year!

SONAR FOR NOTABLE INTERACTIONS	RATING AND/OR REFLECTION IN THE MOMENT	HIGHLIGHT IMPLICATIONS AND LEARNINGS
Feedback starts with proactive recognition - 'sonar' pinging to notice even the smallest outcomes, interactions or exchanges around you	Notice when something gives you cause to reflect or evaluate	If what you've seen or heard makes you want to know more, change something or embed a new learning, say so

DEVELOP AN ACTION	TAKE NOTE	SHARE WITH THE TEAM
Generate a couple of actions based on highlighted learnings or implications	Send yourself an email with the colleague's name and date in the subject line. When the time comes to deliver more substantive feedback, the list of interactions and actions will be available for use in appraisal	Ask permission to highlight the reflections and learnings around the feedback. If "no," do NOT use - this is a win for agency. If "yes," you've reframed a potentially critical feedback incident into a positive learning for the team

Micro-appraisal

Source: APS Intelligence, 2021

CHAPTER 10

I Promise to Be Present, and Not Only When I Need You

There is one last promise that should be made directly and personally to each of our colleagues. It is a promise to be truly and fully present while in their presence and a promise to be in their presence consistently, not just when we want or need something from them.

Many of you have likely had the unfortunate experience of feeling used or manipulated by managers or colleagues who conveniently appear in your life only when it benefits them. Their name pops up in your inbox, and you know immediately that some type of request is forthcoming. And yet often, when you approach these same people, there is a good chance you will be begrudgingly received as an unwelcome and inconvenient distraction.

So this is a promise to never be that person. It's a promise to consistently, selflessly seek out and create quality time and meaningful interactions. It's not a promise to throw open your office doors and devote your days to kibitzing with colleagues. Rather, it's a promise to make better use of the time you have. A promise to forge true connections that contribute to a climate of collegiality because teammates that are familiar with each other and authentically collegial toward one another are proven to perform better.

Making good on this promise starts with an ongoing practice of functional mindfulness. And, again, the mention of "mindfulness" should not evoke images of incense candles or chanting monks. That is not what I'm talking about here.

Mindfulness is more than a quirky, spiritual trend; it is essentially about an intentional focus and attention to what you're doing while you're doing it. How many times have you walked into a room and then stood for a moment trying to remember what you were about to do and why you were there? How many times have you picked up your phone for a specific reason, only to fall down a rabbit hole of apps, messages, notifications, and distraction—never ending up doing the task you wanted to do?

How many times has someone spoken to you briefly in a corridor at work or to a group you were a part of on a video conference call, only for you to realize you've heard nothing of the conversation or can't even recall the interaction after the fact?

Without mindfulness, it is too easy to be consumed and overwhelmed by the myriad thoughts and to-dos competing for attention in our brains. The danger here is twofold. First, and most obviously, a cluttered and distracted mind will cause you to miss important nuances and details about people, about events, and about your workplace. But equally if not more damaging is the effect it will have on those around you. What does it tell people about themselves when you can't conduct a conversation with them without glancing at your phone or computer screen? What does it say when they need you and you can't be bothered to physically turn away from what you're doing for even just a moment? It tells them they're unimportant and an imposition; what they have to say is less important and less interesting than what's happening or may happen in a digital box. It says that they are not worth the energy it takes to swivel a chair in their direction.

There are some simple strategies that can be used to ensure that, even when you are busy, you are giving people the access and attention they need. These may feel overly clinical or procedural at first, but they establish ground rules that protect your boundaries without closing you off altogether.

The first is making yourself ever available for brief pockets of "priority interrupt time" (PIT). We've used this to great effect in our workplace, where, at any time, anyone can pop their head into my office and ask if I'm interruptible. If I'm in the middle of something that truly can't wait, then I ask for a few minutes until I can break. Once I'm ready, though, I focus my attention wholly on what they're bringing to the table. The understanding in our office is that PIT sessions should not exceed two minutes. But, during those two minutes, they get all of me and I all of them. And that promise of undivided attention, even for short bursts of time, is invaluable. It sends a message that what is important to you is important to me, even when I'm busy. We use this same technique in this virtual world by sending a message that says "interruptible?" to a colleague and if they reply, they know they aren't committing to a lost afternoon!

If your ability to dedicate focused time where it's needed is impeded by the number of people asking for that time, it may be necessary to encourage more self-sufficiency within your team— not in order to eliminate time with anyone in particular, but to allow for essential time for everyone. For this, the classroom technique of "Three before me" can be a useful approach. Here the idea is that, before requesting priority interrupt time, people should first seek out the answer from three other sources. If the way forward is still unclear after they have spoken to other colleagues and consulted with existing resources, then it's perfectly reasonable to expect that you will be available to assist. But you can filter out some of the questions and problems that arrive at your desk by formalizing the due diligence that should first be performed.

For the record, I don't believe there are "no bad questions." There really are: questions asked of humans that take 0.000036 seconds to produce the answer on a search engine; questions asked and answered in a person's presence before—often multiple times. There are so many other, important if simple, questions that should get mindful responses, so we need to make time for them first.

I love that the "Three before me" technique encourages people to think about colleagues and how they might support each other, but also that it helps everyone to see that there is real expertise in those around them regardless of their title or role. This system isn't designed to eliminate the need for you to be mindful—it's designed to eliminate the excuses you might make for being mindful with colleagues.

Before the days of app-based rideshares, I would sometimes use old-school car services to and from airports—especially when visiting America. I will never forget one driver who illuminated for me the difference that can be made by the smallest tweaks in action and behavior during an interaction. He was holding a sign with my name when I arrived at the terminal, and it was actually spelled correctly, which was rare, as drivers would usually either miss the "h" in John or find some creative way to mangle my surname. But this driver nailed it. And when I declined his polite offer to carry my luggage, he didn't insist upon it or pressure me as drivers sometimes do (after a long flight, I prefer to wheel my luggage as a walking stick of sorts until my legs wake up).

This driver rightly detected that I was weary from travel, and aside from exchanging names and handshakes, he left me to my thoughts as we walked together to his old Lincoln Town Car. When we got there, I saw immediately that he had noted my height in the passenger profile because both front seats were pushed all the way forward to give me maximum space. Most drivers in this situation would not realize that I might need more room until I was already stuffed uncomfortably into the back seat.

As we pulled out of the airport parking lot, he lifted a two-way radio to his mouth and succinctly said "POB" into the mic before returning it to the cradle. I asked what the acronym stood for, and he gave a huge grin. "Passenger on Board," he said. "It means I gots you!"

He did have me, specifically. From the moment that he double-checked the spelling of my name before putting marker to placard, he was preparing for me. Not just any passenger, but for me.

The memory of this otherwise routine interaction has stayed with me for more than a decade. It provided a clear illustration of the impact that can be made simply by putting a little more thought and care into the time you share with others. It doesn't take much, really. With a bit more focus and a few modifications, you can make clear to anyone you engage with that you've *got* them. You're not just occupying the same space and trading words back and forth. You've *got* them. They are safe and valued and heard and seen and appreciated as an individual.

In the days following that airport ride, I resolved to be more thoughtful in my reception of others and to capture the spirit of hospitality and warmth that seemed to come so naturally to the driver. "POB" became something of a mantra that I used as a reminder to myself before heading into meetings and conversations. And, eventually, I fleshed it out and repurposed the acronym to highlight three keys to mindful and meaningful interactions: Preparation, Orientation, and Behavior. Focusing deliberately on these areas helps to ground me and ensures that I am fully present for conversations, whether in person, on video chat, or just on the phone.

Preparation is the forethought applied to mindset, mood, and affect. Before interactions, make a conscious effort to clear your mind of mental clutter and distractions. Think about the person you're engaging with, even if you don't know them well. How do you want that person to feel during your time with them? What would you like them to get out of the conversation?

Then check in on your mood. Are you agitated? Calm? Nervous? Lingering emotions from previous interactions can cloud your thoughts and judgment, so try to wipe that slate as clean as possible before heading into a meeting. And, lastly, be hyperaware of the effect that you may have simply through your demeanor and facial expressions. Not everyone can deftly distinguish moods. So if your neutral face is reflecting, say, fatigue, it could easily be misinterpreted as boredom or exasperation.

Orientation speaks to the message that you'll send simply by the way that you receive someone. If you're meeting in person, don't wait behind a desk for them to come to you. Don't sit fixed to a screen while they wait for your attention or position yourself such that you can keep an eye on your email. And keep the phone out

141

of sight, *entirely*. So many people sit down for a conversation and immediately set the phone within reaching distance. Even when the screen is facing down, it sends an unmistakable message that an interruption could occur at any moment. People should never feel like they're competing for attention with your phone. They should never feel like they're not important enough for you to adjust your orientation and meet them eye to eye.

In this virtual world you will continue to look at people through screens, and I can tell you that the orientation of your attention is just as important here. I never look at my screen when talking to virtual rooms or meetings. I am looking at each individual face, flipping through multiple screens of tiled faces if I must, to make sure everyone knows that I've got *them*—not a display.

The final piece to think about is your **behavior**—the physical cues that will help you to maintain focus and signal that your attention is fully in one place. Maintaining eye contact is, of course, crucial, but so is your posture and gestures. If your subject appears uncomfortable or nervous, how will you set them at ease? Mirroring is one strategy to alleviate that kind of tension. By subtly replicating the gestures and posture of the person before you, you can create an atmosphere more favorable to building rapport.

The move to more agile working means a change in how we behave online—we need to hold our smile, nods, or shakes of the head longer so people can scan a sea of faces and see your happiness, approval, or dissent, not just tiles of empty stares.

Preparation, orientation, and behavior—it's a mantra that should whisper in your ear leading up to and during each and every interaction. Perhaps that seems so obvious as to be ridiculous. Or perhaps you don't think that you need to be that conscientious and deliberate because you're good at your job, you've been at it a long time, and you know your people quite well. That can work against you, though! Competence often takes us away from mindfulness. And when you are intimately acquainted with the people and processes around you, it's easy to become complacent.

"POB—I've got you." Every time.

Equally as important as being present with people is being present with them *consistently*—not only during formal, scheduled meetings or times when you need something. Our attention is fickle. All over the place with a life of its own, similar to libido. And, to some extent, we are powerless against what grabs it. If you're walking down the street minding your own business and pass a circus clown reading a newspaper on a bench with no pants on, that will capture your attention, at least for a moment.

But inattention is purposeful. What we choose *not* to pay attention to—and who we choose not to pay attention to—tells a clearer story about our priorities and what we value. And one of the worst mistakes you can make as a giant is to use your inattention as a weapon. You should be a familiar presence for your people. You should check in on them often and you should ask them how they're doing, and you should mean it. You should always have some sense of how they're doing both inside and outside of the workplace. That doesn't mean that you pry or you micromanage their psychological state. This is not a promise to intrude on personal lives, but it is a promise to be engaged with people enough to notice when something is off.

Part of this is a concern about safety and wellness. It is not our job to solve every problem. But leaders are sign posters. It is our job to identify problems and either address them or, when appropriate, direct them to people who can help, be that HR or a direct manager.

In the context of this promise, however, the focus of concern is performance. Remember, thriving and performing at our highest level possible is the driving motivation behind all of these promises. And noncompulsory communication—communication that happens outside the formal settings and may not even immediately relate to work—breeds an intimacy that is a hallmark of successful teams. In groups—even in groups of elite individuals—communication is often perfunctory and functional. You do it when you have to. Coworkers are essentially treated as points in a Gantt chart that interact with each other primarily when they need something.

True teams don't operate that way. They use noncompulsory communication all the time. That isn't to say people are sitting in Slack channels all day exchanging pet pictures and Netflix recommendations with their colleagues. Or floating from workstation to workstation to chat about weekend plans. But they do find ways to connect with each other in authentic collegial relationships. They keep in touch consistently and unselfishly.

In 2010, researchers reported a connection between actual touch and team success in the NBA. Led by Michael Kraus, a postdoctoral researcher at the University of California, studied each of the 30 teams for one game early in the 82-game season, documenting every instance that a player engaged in noncompulsory touch.[1] They tracked fist bumps and low fives and butt slaps and the times that a player held a teammate's shoulder while conspiring during a dead ball. So this wasn't in-action, in-game contact like nudging a teammate to the right spot on the floor or falling on them. Rather, it was voluntary touch in the huddle or during substitutions; it was helping a teammate off the floor. It was functional but noncompulsory touch intended to connect, intended to say, "POB, I've got you!"

After the season, the researchers compared the individual and team touch metrics from that early one-game sample against their overall season performance. They were able to control for preseason expectations, player salaries, and team record at the time of the sample game. And, however they sliced it, they found that touch enhanced both individual and team performance. Touch benefited everyone. It signaled cooperative behavior, and it built trust. Not surprising, I suppose, but remarkable, nonetheless.

Small touches yield disproportionately large results. Which is not a call to start slapping butts. That would be problematic. But every culture and every person within that culture has their own love language. A way in which gestures of love are given and accepted. NBA players show their appreciation and camaraderie through high fives and pats on the butt. They use pleasantly profane words of affirmation to encourage and uplift each other. That is their love language.

Our challenge as leaders is to find ways to touch people using the love language they respond to. There are so many ways to do this. You can stop waiting until end-of-year appraisals to give purposeful feedback. That's touch. You can take someone aside after a meeting and thank them for their specific contribution. That's touch. You can look them in the eye and tell them specifically how their job performance has made a difference to the organization—and, on a very basic level, we can ask how they've been getting on and care about the answer. That's touch.

You can give a small gift on special occasions or handwrite a note. You can reach out to someone's manager when you observe behavior that is worthy of kudos. These are all ways to touch. And people respond differently to all kinds of touches, but the common thread is that they all benefit from touch. They benefit from you being around and they benefit from being around each other, provided you're speaking their language.

By promising to be present more frequently, you are promising to create the touchpoints that contribute to a culture of familiarity, an underappreciated quality that has proven to be integral to team success. Researchers have demonstrated across industries the connection between familiarity and effectiveness. In a study of software developers, teams with more experience together completed projects with fewer defects, adhered more closely to budgets and deadlines, and received more favorable client feedback. The amount of time that teammates had worked together was more predictive of performance than were the individual experiences of each team member.[2] In the article reporting this study, authors Robert S. Huckman and Bradley Staats cite similar insights supporting the value of familiarity.[3] Evidence shows that fatigued but familiar flight crews are less error-prone than better-rested but less familiar crews. In fact, the majority of commercial aviation incidents take place during a crew's first flight together. Similarly, in healthcare, surgeons who work in more than one hospital have shown variance in their performance levels, perhaps correlating with how familiar they are with each the support teams at each location.

If we're not careful, of course, a certain type of familiarity can create conditions for laziness. Cruising on autopilot through familiar motions discourages mindfulness and lulls you into taking people for granted. And sticking to the familiar in a way that excludes people or ideas is obviously counterproductive.

But the familiarity that results from being present builds trust. It encourages innovation. It fosters an environment where people interact informally and exchange random ideas that have the potential to coalesce and grow into new and exciting directions. It creates a whole that is greater than the sum of its parts. So that, even if one person leaves, the bonds that connect the group remain durable enough to bridge the gap.

In the following set of promises, we will further explore the ways that we contribute to organizational culture. But before we do that, spend some time reflecting on these last few promises and the state of your relationships with colleagues.

Activity: You and Your Colleagues

Consider the following questions and make some notes on your answers so you can look back at them from time to time to make sure you are keeping your promises.

- What is the image that you're reflecting back when your colleagues look at you? What effect is that having on them?
- What might you unlock if you were to look at them and see something more? If you were to imagine them unbound by the limits of expectations or job descriptions?
- How much time and effort are you spending to help people get better? Are you giving feedback in a way that makes a difference? Are you giving feedback at all? Or do you believe yourself too busy to point out the toilet paper on their shoe?
- Are you present for them? As often as you should be? Enough to build that critical intimacy and familiarity?

Every individual possesses a world of possibilities. And every interaction we have is a chance to tap into that possibility. Commit to connecting. Commit to enhancing people's performance and making them feel good about themselves. Those people—and your relationships with them—will be the difference between good and great. They will be the key to achieving success and the key to avoiding failure. But it starts with you. To be their best, they need your best. And they deserve it.

CHAPTER 11

I Promise to Bear Responsibility for Driving the Culture

There seems to have been a renewed focus on organizational "culture" in recent years—a recognition, perhaps, that something has gone awry in our workplaces and institutions. People have become disconnected and disillusioned. We have grown accustomed to corruption and misbehavior, and we cynically accept benefit reductions, longer hours, and dehumanizing treatment as the new norm. There is broad acknowledgment that organizational culture is in decline, and it must be restored in order to right the ship.

The COVID-19 pandemic and indeed moments of awareness around things like #MeToo, Black Lives Matter, refugee crises, and burgeoning employee activism around climate change and information privacy and security have meant that, from boardrooms to classrooms, people are having to talk about and address the impact of culture.

That is all well and good, but when I sit with corporate leaders, there is often an air of detachment between their influence and the culture they are seeking to improve. They speak about organizational culture in ethereal terms, as if it is separate from them as individuals—larger than them and mostly beyond their sphere of control. What they can do, they seem to believe, is essentially limited to procurement. They can buy a breakfast spread a few days a week or a Ping-Pong table for the break room. They can pay a specialist to talk about diversity or to lead group meditation sessions. They can acquire plug-and-play solutions and hope for the best.

But this is a gross misunderstanding and a dangerous abdication of responsibility. Strategic investments and intentional efforts in cultural reform have their place, yes. But, ultimately, culture is the accumulation of millions of choices made by each colleague.

People make choices. And those choices make culture.

People don't like to believe that culture can be defined, perhaps fearing that, if defined, it may have to be taken more seriously. I heard a consultant speak on this in a virtual panel. He confidently proclaimed: "Culture is impossible to define. It's like smoke. You know it's there, but it's impossible to grasp."

I actually clapped when I heard this—his presentation was perfect—I was watching a true master of the snake oil arts. Everything he said sounded so plausible but was complete bollocks. You can't define culture the same way you define a revenue target or another transaction, but you can understand it and its impact on the experience of our colleagues.

It *is* the product of people's choices. Some people are more influential than others but everyone makes a difference.

People make choices. Choices make culture.

At the other end of the spectrum from those senior leaders, members of the rank and file express an even stronger sense of helplessness. How can they have a meaningful impact on culture when they lack the standing to even sign off on that round of muffins and juice? From their modest spot in the org chart, how can they address concerns around inclusion and diversity and fairness? There are systemic forces that shape culture, as they see it, and they are all but powerless to influence those forces.

But this, too, is wrong. And this, too, abdicates responsibility. Culture is systemic, but it is also intensely and deeply personal. It is everyday people making everyday choices about how they treat one another. And those choices define the experience of a culture.

Dismissing our immediate and actual connection to culture is an indulgence that passively encourages bad behavior. When we excuse ourselves from responsibility for the culture, its more insidious and negative elements become easier to accept or at least overlook. When we choose not to act in the face of small infractions, those infractions become more common and grow in significance. And, over the course of time, the behavior becomes normalized as "part of the culture." As if there was never a time when anything could have been done about it. As if the culture was always this way and always would be.

When looking at organizational cultures a way to define them might be to understand that it is not the most common behaviors in a culture that define them, rather it's the worst behaviors tolerated. Anytime someone in a company, or indeed in society, sees that a nonoptimal behavior goes unsanctioned and sometimes is rewarded, the culture resets to that new baseline of behavior—behavior that (usually) makes life easier for an individual or requires no personal change, but diminishes the organizational performance or colleague experience.

Culture is defined by the worst behaviors tolerated.

Cast your eyes across the institutions of society, from politics to business and beyond, and the examples are clear.

Take, for example, the culture of sports, which are beloved by millions of fans and participants. We root wildly for our favorite clubs and extol the most skilled athletes as heroes. We praise any demonstration of the values that sport claims to espouse—fairness, teamwork, discipline, hard work, sportsmanship, toughness—and we begrudgingly accept the less attractive realities of what sport has become. We might "tsk-tsk" individual actions, but for the most part we've grown to expect a healthy dose of bad with good, and we collectively acknowledge that the bad stuff is just an inherent part of the games we love. It is easier to resign to the belief that it's all just part of the culture of sport and thus unchangeable.

We write off violations of sport's professed values. We tolerate influences within sport that work against the best interests of its primary stakeholders—the athletes and the fans. And all of this starts at the earliest stages of an athlete's development. Youth sports are littered with problems that are evident in plain sight:

overbearing and hypercompetitive parents living vicariously through their progeny; coaches who are ill-equipped to develop children and whose primary qualification is having been decent at the sport a long, long time ago; overspecialization and the proliferation of "elite" or "travel" teams that are financially motivated to recruit children long before such competition is beneficial. Any sideline parent will testify to the reality of these problems, and yet most feel helpless against them. It is simply the culture of youth sports.

The noxious strains within sporting culture are even more apparent and readily accepted at the college level, particularly in the US, where notwithstanding more recent changes that allow small "living stipends" for their supposedly amateur participants, the $1bn-revenue National Collegiate Athletic Association has created an atmosphere that still exploits young adults in a manner that resembles a modern-day plantation – food, lodging and "an education" in return for a schedule that I can tell you from experience is akin to that of a professional athlete on top of the rigours of academia, and all that with severe restrictions on how an individual participant can actually benefit from their skills. It's worth noting that the National Bureau of Economic Research found that less than 7 percent of the revenue generated by National Collegiate Athletic Association—more than $8 billion annually—actually went to the athletes through scholarships and living stipends.[1] Would-be student athletes are denied not only fair compensation for their contributions to their institution but compensation even from holding a part-time job, which is prohibited. Their performance in the classroom is generally an afterthought, with the primary goal being to meet relatively low academic standards required to maintain eligibility. Little attention is given to preparing them for life after sports, which for most will begin when they play their last college game. They are pawns in a high-stakes game, where the only winners are the university coffers and coaches who enjoy high salaries, endorsement deals, the agency to come and go as they please, and a cult-like following on campus.

This is not an environment that puts the young adult first. This is an environment that unsurprisingly leads to academic scandals and worse. It is an environment where sycophants and boosters pledge devotion to the program that blinds them to clues when something is dangerously awry. When fake grades are being handed out en masse. When an extensive network of coaches is engaging in co-ordinated bribery, embezzlement, and corruption. When an assistant coach is sexually assaulting young children whom he is publicly lauded for mentoring. When a highly regarded trainer is raping the athletes he is paid to protect. This is all part of the culture.

There is a racist element to sporting culture, evident in the slurs and chants hurled from the stands and the deficiency of minority representation in ownership, management, and coaching staffs. There is a homophobic element to sporting culture, often attrib-uted too exclusively to participant athletes from backgrounds that are less tolerant of the LGBTQ+ community.

There is a corrosive battlefield culture in sport. A misplaced reverence for the single-minded warriors who power through injury, even at the risk of long-term health, for the sake of victory. Acceptance of this battlefield culture leads to behavior that would be considered abjectly ridiculous in almost any other context. It allows coaches to berate and bully in the name of motivation, to name-call and harass without sanction because it supposedly makes the athlete stronger. Imagine if a language professor at university treated a student athlete the way that many celebrated coaches do. If the professor got in the student's face, close enough for the student to feel spittle and hot breath, and screamed, "Conjugate the fucking verb! How many times do we have to tell you to conju-gate the fucking verb?!?!"

A couple of years ago, footage from a relay marathon in Japan started popping up on my social media feeds. The people sharing the posts were all expressing similar sentiments of awe and rever-ence for the bravery and heroism displayed by the runner featured in the clip. She was a 19-year-old university student named Rei

Lida, and toward the end of her 2.2-mile stretch, she tripped and fractured her right leg. The video shows her teammate waiting about 700 feet away, as Lida perseveres through pain and agony and crawls the remainder of the way, rubbing her knees bloody against the pavement. When she finally gets there and passes off the baton, she attempts to stand but crumbles back to the ground.

"Amazing grit and determination," one viewer wrote. "Her strength and determination is beyond words!" said another. "NEVER underestimate the heart of a true champion."

These comments are, frankly, insane—reflections of, and contributions to, a culture that is all too eager to celebrate this warrior mentality. It's a mentality that puts the warrior at risk of potentially catastrophic consequences in exchange for what are ultimately trivial rewards. These warriors are often their own worst enemy in this regard. They cannot help themselves, and sadly they are enabled and cheered on even by stakeholders who will not have to live with the long-term repercussions. That's how sports are, though. It's part of the culture.

But these aren't problems of culture. They're problems of choices. They're the result of people up and down the ladders of power making choices. People make a choice to award tournament hosting honors to countries that oppress women and are violently intolerant of LGBTQ+ rights. Someone chooses not to correct an uncle at holiday dinner when he wildly misrepresents Colin Kaepernick's message and intentions. People choose to make the university football coach the highest-paid "public servant" in the state. In the meaningless youth soccer game, when someone yells at the teenage umpire, that is a choice. When no one *does* anything about it—*that's* the culture.

"Sport" is not intrinsically anything. It's not homophobic or macho or racist by nature. It can be whatever we want it to be with a bit of good leadership and better choices all around. Different choices will yield different results.

I bang on about this in the context of sport because it provides an obvious example. Collectively, society has decided that, while it is mostly a net positive force, the culture of sport bears irreconcilable flaws that are as old as time and will always be part of the game. We take the good with the bad and underestimate (often willingly) the choices we could make to move the needle in a better direction, even just a nudge.

This happens in the workplace as well. The actual contributors to culture are adept at distancing themselves from its quality. When my APS colleagues and I meet with organizations, we often survey managers anonymously and ask if they believe their own behavior is congruent with the cultural values of the business. And typically, about 80 percent respond, "Yes, my behavior lives up to the cultural values." But when we ask the same group if the behavior of *others* in the organization is congruent with its values, only 30 percent say yes. And 70 percent say, "No, the behavior of my colleagues does not live up to our values."

Now I try to stay in my lane as a psychologist, and arithmetic is not my forte. But it doesn't take a mathematician to recognize that these numbers indicate a troubling disconnect. There appears to be a consensus agreement that the majority of people are contributing positively to culture. But who that majority represents is unclear—because 80 percent of those respondents are saying that other managers, but not themselves, are primarily responsible for the nonoptimal culture within their own organization. They're essentially saying, "It's not me—it's *them*."

It *is* them, though. Because everyone is part of the problem, just as everyone can be part of the solution. No one gets to wash their hands of that commitment. We are all custodians of the culture, and as giants we must promise never to turn our backs on that responsibility. It is the choices that each of us makes that shape the culture around us.

I live across the street from a few small office buildings. From my balcony, I can see down to the courtyard, where employees spend breaks looking at their phones or chatting with colleagues. There are a fair number of smokers among them, and occasionally they'll finish their cigarette and, without a thought, give it that little flick toward the curb. And the butt will land and roll around a bit, sadly burning itself down to the filter as the owner returns to the building.

In every case, someone witnesses this happen, and even those who are momentarily taken back by this minor social indiscretion, do *nothing*. Sometimes two people will see it and they'll share a mournful, but helpless look with a fellow witness. The cigarette butt will be there—inches from their collective feet—but they shrug and they tut silently, and then they too will return to the building or otherwise go about their business.

That is the culture of this courtyard space, and far beyond apparently. Its regular visitors have made the choice to be OK with leaving a little rubbish around.

After all, it's an overreaction to intervene when the offence is so small as to be invisible from a distance, right?

I watch over the course of a week as a few cigarette butts on a Monday are joined by empty juice bottles and sandwich wrappers by Wednesday and, by Thursday, some cardboard that didn't quite make it to the garbage can and a mattress that someone couldn't be bothered taking to the tip. On Friday, at their first break, a person finishes their cigarette and, seeing that such a thing as a cigarette butt couldn't make the mess in the courtyard any worse, they toss theirs into the pile.

Minutes later, there is a burning mattress in the courtyard. Now *everyone* is exercised. They stare from windows; some leave the building and surround the bonfire, scolding the air: "Who did this? How did this happen? Who's going to deal with this?"

Now, rightly, they are suggesting the problem is too big for them to solve, and they want to know when the authorities will come. And when they do: fire trucks or cleaners from one or more offices with buckets and mops and brushes to sweep it all away, you can see people leaving the offices at the end of the day, nodding with approval, murmuring, "This is how it should be."

It's an instructive metaphor to watch unfold week after week. Because inside so many workplaces, the exact same dynamic is at play. Someone drops a bit of rubbish in the form of a seemingly minor or fleeting indiscretion—a missed opportunity; an inappropriate or uncharitable comment—and we tell ourselves it's nothing major, just a scrap. Someone will pick it up, to be sure.

But once a few scraps start blowing around, people get used to it. Once it becomes clear that leadership has chosen to tolerate a bit of rubbish, people feel safer in the choice to leave their own behind. And, unattended, the rubbish will accumulate faster than those sidewalk butts. A professional (HR or the legal team) may be able to intervene and clean the mess temporarily, but, unless the choices change, the culture will stay the same and the rubbish will return.

No one gets a pass to walk past the rubbish. When you see something, you must do something. What you choose to do will differ depending upon your place in the organization. But everyone can do something. Everyone owns some responsibility for the culture.

When I speak of accountability this way, it is sometimes perceived as a call for dramatic or revolutionary action. A challenge to spit in the face of authority or to lay across the tracks and refuse to budge until your righteous demands are met. That is not what this promise demands. Raging against the machine is not required. Most people cannot afford the luxury of sacrificing or jeopardizing their job when it fails to meet their standards for fairness and what is right. And there may well be times when the litterbug is too powerful to be dealt with directly. But everyone can pick up the litter. It doesn't have to be confrontational. Returning to the youth athletic fields, for example, you don't have to confront the parent who berates the young umpire, but you can certainly take a minute after the game to offer the umpire some kind words and express your gratitude for their work.

Similarly, when you observe offensive or negligent behavior in the workplace, you can treat its casualties. You can make clear to people that you are aware of what's going on and that they are not alone. You can demonstrate your commitment to the culture with every choice you make in your interactions with people—with the way that you greet them and shake their hands and look at them with curiosity and acceptance. There are so many people in our workplaces who are afflicted by loneliness or insecurity or anxiety, and their ability to get through a day can be dramatically enhanced by incidental but authentic interactions with people who truly see them. They face the day with a sense of dread for all the rubbish that will be strewn their way. But if they can count on one smiling face that will warmly and sincerely ask how they're doing, it can make a world of difference. It can be a life raft through choppy waters.

At the client sites that I visit, I habitually go out of my way to interact with so-called "service workers"—the security guards, the receptionists, the cleaning staff—the people with the least power. I want them to know that I *see* them, because in most organizations these people are considered fringe actors, largely replaceable and virtually invisible. If there is a working lunch, these anonymous workers will descend on the conference room and lay out drinks and platters of food and disposable flatware and utensils. And their presence will hardly register with the more important folk who are conducting real business. There is nary a nod as the crew comes and goes. They are the grease in the gears, but not an actual gear. Because that is how people have *chosen* to view and treat them. In many workplaces, that has become the culture.

I find that abhorrent, so I choose to act otherwise, especially when senior leaders are present. I will be the one to stop the lunch meeting and thank the delivery crew, and I'll make eye contact with each one so that they know they've been seen. It doesn't take long to do, and it's not subversive or defiant. It's just a public demonstration of how I believe people should be treated, even if it is at times awkward or inconsistent with office norms. Even if is contrary to the existing culture.

Everyone has the power to pick up cigarette butts, and everyone shares the job. That may not sit right with you; you may find it unfair. You didn't leave those butts on the ground, after all. And it's not your job to go around picking up other people's trash.

Plus, you are probably so conscientious otherwise. You recycle and compost and pick up after yourself. And even if you did agree to pick some up, what would be the point, you might ask. There will always be more added to the pile.

If that is your mindset, a quick and severe adjustment is in order. Whether you are the CEO or one of the aforementioned service-level workers, you are a custodian of the culture. And you must promise to honor that commitment.

People make choices. Choices make culture.

What are the choices that you made today? And what choices will you make tomorrow? The answers to those questions matter. Don't kid yourself to believe they don't.

CHAPTER 12

I Promise to View the Organization Critically and Truthfully

I read a lot of corporate mission statements and "We Believe" lists. It's part of my job, but it's also grown to be a sick addiction of sorts. In that way, it's like Twitter, I suppose. I start reading with innocent intent, but predictably I fall down some rabbit hole of rhetorical horror that invariably leaves me feeling worse than when I logged on.

In the case of the mission statements, I'm usually trying to gain some familiarity with a prospective client or a client competitor. And, while doing so, I'll come across a bit of text that is so patently ridiculous or delusional that I can't help but do an internet search for the "About Us" or "Who We Are" pages for every business in the industry to see if they've written something comparably maddening. Almost always, they have.

The vast majority of organizations have a sizable gap between what they promise publicly and what they deliver in reality. In Chapter 11, we looked at corrosive elements within the culture of sport, but how is that reality described by its most powerful institutions? In the USA, the National Federation of Stage High School Associations (NFSHSA) is a leading advocate for "education-based high school athletics." Its "We Believe" declaration includes a long list of what the NFSHSA believes athletics *does*. It "promotes respect, integrity, and sportsmanship." It "prepares for the future in a global community." But, oddly, the final point on the list—one that I would think is rather important—is qualified only as a *should* and not a does. Athletics "should be fun," it suggests, rather tepidly.

Hop over to the site of the National Collegiate Athletic Association (NCAA), and you'll find its three core "priorities" prominently displayed: "ACADEMICS, WELL-BEING, FAIRNESS." The actual athletics themselves are apparently an incidental construct designed to support these more sacred priorities. In fact, NCAA bylaws explicitly state that "student participation in intercollegiate athletics is an *avocation*." An avocation? It's an odd choice of word, no? Merriam-Webster.com defines "avocation" as (1) "a subordinate occupation pursued in addition to one's vocation especially for enjoyment: HOBBY" or (2) "customary employment: VOCATION."[1] Ask anyone who has participated in "amateur sport" in any way and at any level whether it was treated as a "hobby," and I strongly suspect they'll say no. But the second definition doesn't work either, because clearly the NCAA would have us believe that academics, not athletics, represents the student athlete's "customary employment" or vocation. And further, athletics can't be an occupation or vocation in this context because those things pay a wage. ACADEMICS, WELL BEING, and FAIRNESS. That's what the NCAA is all about, it would have you believe. The games and tournaments happening in the background are not a multimillion dollar industry. They're just a precious "avocation."

On the FIFA website, the disciplinary code has recently been updated to add protections for gay and lesbian athletes. It promises severe sanctions for "any person who offends the dignity or integrity of ... a person or group of people through contemptuous, discriminatory, or derogatory words or actions ... on account of race, skin colour, ethnic, national or social origin, gender, disability, sexual orientation, language, religion, political opinion, wealth, birth or any other status or any other reason."[2] This is the same FIFA that is preparing for the 2022 World Cup in Qatar, a country where practicing homosexuality is punishable by death.

Principles and values appear to be negotiable when awarding hosting rights. Certainly, that's a philosophy shared by the

International Olympics Committee (IOC). The Olympics are billed as the pinnacle of the sporting ethos, and the IOC mission prattles on about placing "sport at the service of the harmonious development of humankind, with a view to promoting a peaceful society concerned with the preservation of human dignity." It's difficult to imagine, however, how that comported with awarding the 2014 Games to Russia as they were threatening their neighbors and passing hostile legislation to silence and stifle its LGBTQ+ community. Or how China will be preserving human dignity in 2022 when they host the Games for the second time in less than 20 years, as more than a million Muslim ethnic minorities sit in detention camps.

I think it's important here to pass on a significant learning I've gained from travel: never conflate the government of any country with the people of a country.

I've mentioned some governments here, and in recent times the governments of the UK and USA along with some in the EU could easily be added to lists of those committing unconscionable acts, from the *Windrush* scandal in the UK to caged refugee children in the USA. All the people in these countries aren't "bad," but some of the actions of their governments (and mine) bring us shame.

Nonetheless, these examples are stark illustrations of an incongruence that runs just as rampant in the business world. There is a pathological disconnect between the stories that we tell about our workplaces and the actual experiences of people within them. Some of the cleverer organizations avoid stating untruths by projecting aspirational mission statements: declarations of what is hoped for at some later date, rather than assessments of the present state. This is particularly true around matters of diversity and inclusion. It's pleasant and easy to talk about the rosy rainbow future, where we will all be judged by the "content of our character" and where we will work together productively in peace and harmony. Thus, many organizations focus on that utopian tomorrow because where they are today is far less inspiring.

But most organizations seem less concerned about putting forth false narratives. Their mission statements and "About Us" pages describe a world where every individual is cherished and supported and given equal opportunities to grow and develop. Using different words, they recruit prospective employees by making many of the same promises that I've asked you to make. But when those prospective employees become actual employees, they quickly learn they've been sold a bill of goods. And before long, they leave or start planning their exit strategy, leaving us to wonder, *How could they? These Millennials, they're so flighty! They want everything!* They don't want everything, though. They only want the experience you said you were offering them.

Now, I'm not naïve enough to expect organizations to project a perfectly objective reality of who they are. That could get quite ugly in some cases. But *you* cannot buy into your organization's hype—especially if you care about improving it. Leadership (and again I mean colleagues demonstrating it as well as named managers displaying it) requires a clear and accurate assessment of the landscape. It requires the same scrutiny that I asked you to direct inward in the very first promise (Chapter 1). Just as you promised there to view yourself critically and truthfully, you must promise here to view your organization critically and truthfully.

You can think about it in the context of mental contrasting. It's necessary to have a clear and specific vision for the rosy future that you see for your organization. But you will never get there without a pragmatic assessment of the "now" that is as transparent and vivid as the future that you're aiming to achieve. So this is a promise to be clear-eyed about the now, about the true nature of our people and our teams. It's a promise to be more precise with how we describe ourselves, to stop feigning ignorance of the way things really are.

It's a promise to acknowledge the absence of meritocracy, the presence of mediocrity, and the need for change to reach those ideals. There is solid research suggesting that positive change to optimize performance and colleague experience does not start until people come to terms with the fact that their organization is not functioning optimally—including the fact that it is *not* a meritocracy.

I can all but assure you that your organization is not that. To believe otherwise is to believe that any homogeny and inequality that exist are merely the results of one type of people being functionally better at the job than another. When I enter a boardroom filled with high-level executives who are predominantly white and male, I always ask them to wonder, "What are the chances?" What are the chances that the very best brains for these jobs are all sitting in the heads of white men?

The idea of a meritocracy is fine as long as it's recognized as an aspiration and not the existing status quo. We must promise to see reality as it is and acknowledge that ineffectiveness from leaders and a lack of systemic scrutiny—intentional or not—has over time created an unlevel playing field. If we deny this truth, any of the work that is done to improve the situation will be miscast by skeptics as "social engineering," "positive discrimination," or worse.

One key obstacle on the path to meritocracy—or any type of forward progress, really—is the undeniable prevalence of mediocrity within our ranks. I want to be clear here that I don't mean people who are new or learning their craft, or those adapting to a new role or experiencing internal or external challenges that impact their performance. I am talking about people who *could* be exceptional but choose to be average. Some have done so because they can get away with delivering little with no consequence. Others because they are sophisticated and tenured and they know the business well enough to hide. Others are poorly managed and disenchanted and now unable to deliver at their highest expectations.

There are more reasons still, but before you accuse me of cruelty here, just remember we have names for this group—we call them the "permafrost" or the "marzipan layer," a group of people who have perfected the maxim of giving "just enough" but never as much as possible. We know this makes up an often disproportionately large number of people, and, whether a function of apathy, mismanagement or anything else, we know it harms our organization.

"Just enough" might be enough sometimes. But competing and winning in a world that is only growing more disrupted and challenging by the day requires more. It requires the absolute best of people. It requires us to live up to the grand and powerful words that we deploy, often carelessly. I regularly hear people point to examples of "leadership" that are in truth just examples of "resource management." We say "colleagues" when what we really mean is "coworkers." "Colleague" suggests a camaraderie, a shared vision. People who merely orbit around each other in a Gantt chart and programmatically trade emails back and forth all day are not "colleagues." They are "coworkers."

It's important that you get this language right because doing so makes it harder to indulge in a fantasy about the state of your organization. Are your people really "collaborating"? Or are they actually "project-working" or, worse, "sharing a whiteboard"? Sometimes executives give the impression that collaboration is as simple as having an open floor plan. But collaboration is so much more. It's an equal partnership combining support and challenge. It's a mutual purpose for the betterment of the entire organization. It's about contributing even when it's not convenient or in your immediate best interest. It's fueled not only by extrinsic reward but by intrinsic motivation. And collaboration is proactive, not reciprocal. Keeping score of who owes what is not part of collaboration—it's not scratching other people's backs so that they'll scratch yours. Rather, it's about anticipating the need for support and providing it persistently, even if it's initially declined. As we've said before, collaboration is a key part of teaming, and teaming is a perpetual state of calculated selflessness.

Teams collaborate; they don't project-work. But don't assume that you have teams in your organization because that's another word that is habitually misused. When people speak about teams, more often than not they are really speaking about groups of individuals. These groups range in cohesiveness and effectiveness, from self-directed workers bound only by common tasks to fully optimized teams that truly operate as a unit. Between them, the continuum includes nominal groups, high-functioning groups, and emergent teams.

When I meet with organizations, I will sometimes share this spectrum of groups and ask which they feel best describes them. The overwhelming majority of respondents, answering anonymously, place themselves in that high-functioning group category—not because it's true or actual, but because the middle of any range is the safest place to be. Placing yourself any lower on the scale would be an indictment of the organization, and everybody knows that anything higher is extraordinarily unlikely. So, rather than take an honest, critical view, most people choose to believe their "teams" fall in this safe space of "high-functioning group"—a space where the end results are just fine and, conveniently, the impetus to improve is negligible.

While the high-functioning group is always the most popular response, there are usually a few outliers on either end of the scale. The self-identifying self-directed workers reflect a belief that, regardless of what system or matrix they're buried in, they are completely alone. If they have a project that needs support but is not high profile or does not generate revenue, they are alone. If they need to chat through a problem, they are alone. That's what's being felt down at that end. On the opposite end, there is some aspirational fantasy at play. If the vast majority, which is likely grading on a generous scale, can't bring themselves to select one of the two options with "team" in the name, it is highly unlikely that these few stragglers are truly part of an "optimized team" as they claim.

Just like "just enough" may be enough to get you by, "groups" might get you by, too. Although they are limited and perfunctory, coworkers and project working and resource management may be all your organization needs to keep the lights on from day to day. But success and growth through turbulence requires teams, colleagues, collaboration, and leadership. Anything less will be inadequate in the face of heightened competition, geopolitical instability, cyberthreats, digital disruptors, volatile markets, increased automation, and evolving expectations from both your workforce and clientele.

Tectonic shifts are taking place. And to effectively respond to such perpetual and dramatic change, we must be honest about who we are and what we're working with. I have found that, as with groups, there are common character types predictably distributed throughout the workplaces I visit.

I refer to them as the "Six Protagonists": the Vanguards, the Reasoned Believers, the Pessimists, the Apathetic, the Entrenched, and the Insurgents. Members of these clans span all levels of hierarchy, tenure, experience, and technical expertise. If you can identify and understand them, you can tailor their experience to inspire those who are with you, motivate the undecideds, and neutralize the detractors.

The Six Protagonists

Vanguards	Engaged, and leading from the front. See themselves as instrumental in building the organization.
Reasoned Believers	Follow the lead of the Vanguards, but are proactively engaged in building the organization after scrutinizing leaders.
Pessimists	Wondering if their contribution to the organization matters. Have lost faith in the plan and their role in it.
Apathetic	Have stopped worrying if their contributions matter to the organization. They continue to work, but only for the benefit of others.
Entrenched	'Unconscientious objectors' who do the absolute minimum and seek to maintain the status quo while flying under the radar.
Insurgents	Work undercover to pull the rug out and cause a failure of any organizational plan. Vigilant, sophisticated, and invisible to the organization.

There are gray areas, of course, and not everyone fits perfectly into these categories at all times. But these descriptors of the Six Protagonists reflect more than a decade's worth of data and observation collected across four continents and numerous industry sectors. And, in my experience, assessing organizations through the framework of these categories can inform a differential approach that will succeed where one-size-fits-all efforts have failed.

Please note that this isn't a hierarchical list—the Vanguards aren't "better" than the "Reasoned Believers"; they are both essential and some of the other groups are in their particular category through no fault of their own, so reserve judgment as you read on.

The Vanguards

Your most enthusiastic advocates are the Vanguards. These individuals are naturally driven to be at the forefront of logistical and cultural innovation—they want to participate in driving change and be recognized for that, no matter their technical role. They are growth mindset thinkers who don't need to see a mountain of evidence before diving "all in" on proposed changes. But they are not lemmings or run-of-the-mill sycophants. They have a keen sense of organizational incongruence and will expect that what is said within the organization (about everything from standards to values to rules) will closely match reality. If that expectation is met, however, and they feel a consistent and authentic connection to what they see as consistently ethical leadership, then they will not only thrive but will become your most powerful advocates to drive performance and lead the unconverted and unconvinced— with or without actual management titles.

It is best to engage these early adopters during the initial stages of any change initiative. Do not wait until ideas and strategy are fully formed, and then bring them on board and expect them to champion change. They want to hear from their leaders and be heard every step of the way. They need to be part of the action at all times—informed, empowered, trusted, and challenged. And if that need is unmet—if they are made to feel excluded or inconsequential—they can quickly go from Vanguard to Insurgent. Or they can simply choose to leave.

The Reasoned Believers

After the Vanguards are the Reasoned Believers, who in an improved but still realistic world would comprise the majority of an organization. Reasoned Believers are eager and essential followers whose natural skepticism can only be countered by a consistent, congruent experience with the organization, purposeful connections with trusted peers, and at least one tangible and authentic connection with a leader. They don't need to be cued in on every detail of a plan or strategy in order to endorse it. But they do need to believe that any future vision is logical, plausible, well considered, and conceived in the unequivocal best interests of the organization. Their motivation benefits from clear and consistent communication that makes clear the implications of any change or decision. They need the people they trust (usually a combination of named and unnamed leaders) to be transparent with reservations or uncertainties, and they value an open-ended opportunity to give their own feedback and express their own concerns.

If all this happens, the well-led Reasoned Believer will follow with caution but confidence, even tolerating periods of anxiety or personal inconvenience. When it doesn't happen, any absence of support or transparency will be immediately noted and filed away as a systemic organizational flaw. Too many of those in the file, and the Reasoned Believer is likely to descend through the stages that follow, first as a Pessimist.

The Pessimists

Pessimists are former Reasoned Believers who refuse to be fooled again. They've been burned too many times by people or initiatives that failed to deliver on promises of change. They are people who could be motivated by new ideas if they could connect those ideas to an organizational or personal benefit, but they're no longer able to do so. And if a trusted peer or manager cannot make that connection clear, new ideas become associated with stress and anxiety, not the intended excitement.

A small component of the Pessimists are also operating—or believe themselves to be operating—at the upper limits of their expertise. They feel overwhelmed by the job at hand without the additional pressure of relearning aspects of their hard-won knowledge or reengineering a role that they already feel stressed to manage. But their behavior is rarely motivated by malice, and that is the good news. The resistance or obstruction of the Pessimists is a coping mechanism, not defiance. They are eminently reachable. Because it doesn't feel good to be hopeless, and they will be willing to consider ways out of that situation if they are pragmatic, staged and eminently plausible with an eye on those quick wins.

Returning them to the fold takes a steady diet of congruent, consistent, informative, and transparent messaging from the organization. Then it takes action.

It takes support and trust from their direct manager. These individuals, in particular, have lost sight of the "big picture," and any guiding vision seems blurry. For that reason, it's critical to facilitate authentic connections with the Vanguards and the Reasoned Believers. That support element cannot be slandered as "babysitting" or "differential coddling"—again, *the Millennials*! It is a practical and necessary way to bring onside the most easily reached clan that stunts the growth of your organization.

And if you don't "coddle" or "babysit"? The Entrenched and the Insurgents will be happy to fill the void. Left unattended, the Pessimists are highly susceptible to the influence of those two groups. Even tacit connections with them can take root and grow quickly, so explicitly countering that outcome is essential. This is a battle for hearts and minds, pitting those who would lead and follow a path of positive change and those who prefer and profit from continued stagnation.

The Apathetic

I've already mentioned the Entrenched and the Insurgents, but before we take a closer look at them, we must first discuss the Apathetic. Unlike the Pessimists, the Apathetic are not waiting to be shown an escape from hopelessness. They are now actively disengaged—the adult equivalent of rolling up into a ball, shutting your eyes, and sticking your fingers in your ears. Even the Pessimists' passive disengagement and yearning for something better is too energy expensive for the Apathetic. They use apathy as a defense mechanism and believe that, to "do right by their employer," they can only focus on the core responsibilities of their jobs. It's not that they don't care about personal and organizational improvement anymore. For some, it's simply that they feel unable to handle the worry, stress, and feelings of inadequacy that come with the uncertainty of trying something new or different. Others are so disenchanted with the incongruence in the promises of their employer and their own individual experience, and yet feel completely beholden to the security of their position, they've concluded, through simple cost–benefit analysis, that ignoring talk of values, plans for change and the like, and focusing instead on completing work tasks—maybe even to a higher standard—will discourage people from expecting their full participation.

And it is a shame because the Apathetic can be people for whom embracing culture and change might have once been a motivating prospect, even if it now appears a pipe dream, a gamble that more often than not will lead to a personal loss. They would need an absolutely brilliant reason and a clear series of quick wins staring them in the face in order to risk being disappointed and opening old wounds. So they leave anything more than "just enough" to the less senior and more energized members of the organization. The support that they once longed for never arrived, and now that ship has sailed as far as they're concerned.

There is not much good news where the Apathetic are concerned. I cannot offer guidelines for how to successfully rehabilitate them because only brilliant line management and consistency of experience over time will make a difference. The only likely natural affinity they feel is to the Entrenched, who project a certainty and purpose that, while contrary or at least unaligned to the organization's progress, is deeply reassuring.

It is likely that they regularly interact with members of the Entrenched, and there is a good chance they are even managed by one, which has a stupefying effect on personal development and the growth mindset that is required for innovation and resiliency. But attempts to cajole and motivate the Apathetic risk alienating them further and contributing to their victim mentality. Thus, they are a particularly complex group to reach, and trying demands a patience that can seem disproportionate to their individual "value." As is the case for the two remaining groups that follow, the best way to negate the impact of the Apathetic is through actions that slow down their membership pipeline. Because once someone falls into their ranks, it takes remarkable leadership to get them back.

The Entrenched

The Entrenched, alternately known as "the permafrost" or the "marzipan layer," have moved beyond apathy. Their members, sophisticated conscientious objectors with misguided consciences, endeavor to preserve the status quo because it benefits them and because doing otherwise would likely mean extra work, discomfort, and sacrifice. Sadly, in many organizations, this is the most highly populated clan. They are seasoned but unambitious, mediocre, and/ or disengaged workers, and they are adept at gaming the system— true masters and disciples of "just enough." The Entrenched resist change and improvement initiatives, especially those that are cultural or otherwise "tangential" to their job (including, but not limited to, technology updates, mentoring, leadership development, and inclusion efforts). They've learned how to hit only the necessary marks on their appraisals, which they know full well are conducted either by an overextended manager who they've worked with for years or an overextended manager who is a virtual stranger.

Members of this group will not always be easy to identify. It may take the presence of a new senior leader or a considerable organizational transformation to expose them to light for the first time. They can recite the company mission and values by heart and can pass for an engaged employee in calculated scenarios (in front of clients or more senior leaders, for example). But they are all talk and glacial action. They present as industrious, contributing members of the group while behaving in ways that subvert change when not under scrutiny. In senior leadership positions, where you will find many of their ilk, the Entrenched can be high achievers who simply don't fancy the hassle, effort, or accommodation of changes that they've decided will bring them insufficient value for their trouble.

This clan is deeply toxic to organizational culture. Their sheer numbers and the inclusion of influential named managers makes them a powerful force. The tone they set will leech into the organization and become the unwritten norm: they can be the embodiment of the maxim I mentioned in Chapter 11—that your culture is defined by the worst behavior tolerated. This is a group that will both exhibit and tolerate a lot of nonoptimal behavior.

The Entrenched quietly but clearly demonstrate that maximum attainment and drive are only "nice to haves," and they prove that coasting through at least some elements of one's job is not a terminal decision. Because in the back of their minds, members of the Entrenched believe that they will retire or jump ship unharmed before the organization as a whole sinks.

Counterintuitively, increases in stress, competition, and disruption only lures more people toward the Entrenched. Although that group itself is perhaps the greatest existential threat to the organization, its members are seen as survivors. Nonetheless, it is possible, albeit difficult, to win back members of this group. Some of them have simply been seduced by a manager or another friendly face who offered to "show them the ropes" and has led them astray. Many of them know they are not in the right clan, but they need to hear a new voice to bring them back. If they do return, some will do so with a renewed zeal to make up for their misspent moments among the Entrenched.

The Insurgents

The final clan is the Insurgents, who even in the worst environments should make up only a small but significant minority. These are individuals who may have once sought change through acceptable, formal channels, but frustrations over being unheard have sent them off piste. Insurgents are likely to emerge after repeated institutional failures or after a particularly radical period of change (think, post-COVID and after some of the inclusion interventions around Black Lives Matter, for example), and they will rationalize their subversive resistance by rightfully noting the incongruence between the leadership's stated values and the lived experience within the organization. Even when given legitimate opportunities to help move the needle in a positive direction, the Insurgents will opt otherwise, preferring subtle ways to undermine those efforts, alongside sophisticated, covert "grenade throwing" intended to both improve their own circumstances and bring about the end of a regime, strategy, or outcome they believe undeserving of success.

Members of the Insurgents may operate with a few like-minded co-conspirators, but their effectiveness is facilitated largely by the silent complicity of the Entrenched. They are often dangerously well connected and potentially poisonous to impressionable coworkers. But they are rarely heard from and can be difficult to identify. Their effect will be clearer than their identities, though. When organizational initiatives are derailed by unforeseen setbacks, it may well be the work of the Insurgents.

This is the most resource-intensive group to change. At least some of them will be traditionally thought of as high performers who deliver necessary results but whose modus operandi is to quietly suppress change until they are either old or secure enough to retire or prepared for a better or at least parallel role in a new organization. How these individuals are managed will indicate how serious the organization is about true progress.

What you choose to do with a visible and tenured high-performer who is also an insurgent says a lot about the organization you intend to be.

Organizations need the ability to change dynamically and respond with agility. They need to be prescient enough about disruption to adapt as it occurs or even before. But, to achieve that, their leaders must understand in explicit detail the relative proportion and influence of the protagonists in their midst. It might not be possible to radically increase the number of Vanguards or to eradicate all of the Insurgents, but identifying them and taking steps to convert even a fraction of the less desirables to more proactive clans can yield massive dividends.

Research from McKinsey has found that, while insufficient budget is responsible for about 14 percent of failure in company-wide initiatives, internal sabotage is the key factor, consisting of some combination of incongruent manager behaviors (33 percent) and direct and indirect employee resistance (39 percent).[3] What that essentially says is that successful change can come from effectively managing, motivating, and leveraging the people who make up for 72 percent of the potential for failure.

However, you can't motivate them if you don't truly know who they are. You can't think about how to improve collaboration if you're not even defining it accurately within your organization. You can't move toward meritocracy if you believe you're already there.

Promise not to shy away from a critical assessment of your organization. Don't make assumptions about the ability or nature of your workforce or the reality of culture based on subjective readings of employee surveys, productivity scores, client wins, or the highfalutin nonsense you're projecting on your website. It costs nothing but energy to start melting the permafrost. To start turning groups into teams. To start living up to the mission statement. But starting any of that starts with an objective analysis of your starting point. It's a step you cannot afford to skip.

CHAPTER 13

I Promise to Promote Everyday Inclusion Based on Earned Disclosure

A few years ago I was coaching a woman who worked for one of the Big Four professional service firms. By then she'd been a partner for two years, and when I first met her, we had a lovely chat for about an hour and decided, yes, we wanted to work together. But the next time I saw her, something was different when she started speaking and I had to stop her almost immediately. "Excuse me," I said, "You're from Wolverhampton!"

This was only surprising because the first time we had spoken, she wasn't—or at least her accent wasn't. It was one of those generic somewhere-in-central-London accents.

Wolverhampton is a blue-collar town in the English West Midlands, parts of which lie in what is known as the "Black Country." That name harkens back to the 1840s and refers to the soot deposit and air pollution that resulted from the coal mines, factories, and mills that dominated the landscape during its industrial heyday.

People from the region often speak with a distinct dialect and accent called "Black Country Spake." They are generally regarded as a warm and hospitable sort, but not particularly intelligent. Please understand this is not what I think, but I imagine you won't have to have grown up in Wolverhampton, or my own hometown, Stockport, for that matter, to realize that some accents are intrinsically and unfairly associated with the supposedly innate, negative qualities of the people who live in those regions.

In response to my observation, she confirmed that she was indeed from Wolverhampton and that she suppressed the accent in professional interactions—indeed, anytime she left her house. She didn't want to discuss it much more, though, and said it was "no big deal."

I couldn't let it go. "It kind of is a big deal if you have one voice for work and one voice for the rest of your life," I said. "So what's that all about?"

Relenting, she explained that "Women from Wolverhampton don't make partner here." The fact that she had done so was almost as unlikely as a chubby bookworm from Stockport ascending to the NBA. But she had, and to maintain her standing, she clearly believed she had to maintain this façade from the time her front door closed as she began her walk to her local London Underground station in the morning to the time she returned home at night. It cost her an effort, she confessed, that was exhausting.

Imagine the amount of energy that this remarkable woman was spending to avoid arousing suspicion. Imagine the mental toll it took on her day after day. And why, to what end? To sell more product? To better satisfy customers? To lead through disruption? No. None of that. The price she was paying simply allowed her to fit in into an environment that had been socially engineered for homogeneity. The energy she was expending—which could have been dedicated to any number of worthy objectives—was instead spent in the service of a pointless and banal expectation with no relation to organizational success or progress.

Take one moment and consider how much energy it would take you to adopt a different persona—a completely flawless and believable one, complete with backstory. How much energy to create it, maintain it, defend it when challenged, and keep that up with everyone—or at least almost everyone in your life?

People's energy is finite. It can either be focused on the shared goals and objectives of an organization, or it can be split—some towards the goals, others for unnecessary tasks designed to help you blend in. Every fraction of energy syphoned away from performance is lost to it.

This is why a culture of inclusion is so important—it facilitates disclosure and that facilitates organizational performance.

It's an ethical imperative, sure, and, with increased scrutiny over hiring practices, inclusion is also a public relations imperative. But, first and foremost, facilitating disclosure is a performance prerogative. So when I suggest here that you keep this promise to promote everyday inclusion in your workplace, based upon earned disclosure, I do so not because that's the "nice" way to treat people. Rather, it's the *only* way to treat them if you expect to extract all of what they have to offer.

I want to be clear about what I mean by "everyday inclusion" and "earned disclosure," and I'll begin with the former. Inclusion must be the standard because inclusion is a choice that we make, a state that is created and maintained by our actions. Diversity, in contrast, is our collective destiny. In modern society, diversity is inevitable and on the rise. But inclusion is optional—rooted in everyday choices that are made anew daily.

Organizations tend to treat the absence of inclusion with intervention-based approaches. It is a finite and well-packaged problem that, once identified, can be solved in the ways that finite and well-packaged problems are solved: by creating some crude curriculum or training plan with a start date and an end date in the not-too-distant future; by committing a certain percentage of your staff to this inclusion initiative; and maybe even hiring a consultant or a guest speaker. Problem dealt with and solved. Check.

At the risk of shooting myself in the foot, that's not how it works. I have a high regard for the expertise that I offer and, more importantly, for the brilliance of my APS colleagues, but we cannot transplant into your workplace a culture of everyday inclusion. That "everyday" bit is essential, because inclusion is in the minutiae. It's in the dull and the onerous and the monotonous. Most of the "othering" that prevents inclusion is subtle and sophisticated. It is not casual use of insensitive language or direct refusals to work with people who are different in some way, and it cannot be dealt with solely via carefully prepared initiatives stored in shared spreadsheets. Initiatives and spreadsheets will not instill everyday inclusion.

Everyday inclusion is achieved when people feel confident that they are consistently being seen, heard, and valued as whole and unique individuals. There is nothing so isolating as being surrounded by people and yet feeling completely alone. That is the nature of exclusion.

In the early 1990s, the researcher William Kahn introduced the concept of "psychological safety," defining it as the ability "to show and employ one's self without fear of negative consequences to self-image, status, or career."[1] It was further explored in the team context by another researcher, Amy Edmondson, who described it as "a shared understanding that the environment is safe for interpersonal risk-taking."[2]

Psychologically safe teams are not "soft"—they are not places for poor performers to hide from scrutiny. In contrast, they are the most robustly challenging environments where little escapes scrutiny; where people share their nascent ideas fully expecting objective challenge, suggestion, and support in equal measure.

Psychologically safe spaces are unique in that they are spaces where people agree to be personally accountable for their impact on others.

Psychologically safe teams do not conflate the ideas generated by colleagues that end up not passing muster with the people who provided those ideas.

In these spaces, colleagues don't imagine that everyone has to operate in the same way to provide value—even as they recognize that may create moments of tension or friction in the pursuit of excellence.

This psychological safety is essential in an environment of everyday inclusion. Psychologically safe teams provide security and liberate their members to trust in one another; to disclose and offer insights fully in the pursuit of solutions, without fear of repercussion or humiliation.

The matter of disclosure is one of the most misunderstood aspects of inclusion.

The act of "coming out" is primarily associated with revelations about sexuality. But coming out happens anytime someone puts forth new or at least little-known information about themselves without being certain of how it will be received.

There are few things more precious to us than our own identities—complex and layered as they are—and when we share a less obvious piece of our identity, it's as if we're presenting a Fabergé egg to a stranger. We're offering a delicate, invaluable truth, and, once it's offered, we have no control over what is done with it. All we can hope is that people treat it with the same amount of care that we do.

People believe that when someone tells you something about themselves, you are learning something about them, but that's wrong—or at least incomplete. Voluntary, "earned disclosure" is always as much a statement about the person receiving the information as it is about the person offering it. Earned disclosure is a profound statement about the recipient that says: "I have watched how you behave and listened to how you talk, and you have earned my trust enough that I believe that I can give you this piece of me and you will treat it with the same dignity and care as I do myself." That trust—the ability to be vulnerable—is so powerful for organizational bonding.

Successful teams require such earned disclosure. They require leaps of faith, but they also assure their members that their faith is well placed. They require that people trust, not because reciprocation is bound to come or mandated to come, but because the natural order is that trust begets trust. This can be achieved only in a culture where personal disclosure never leads to sanction, ridicule, or marginalization, and indeed where admitting to an error in good faith doesn't mark you for life. Teams cannot thrive when their members are preoccupied with worries that what makes them unique will be exploited or mocked if made public.

This freedom to be our complete selves in the workplace is often thought of as gratuitous—one of those warm and fuzzy "nice to haves." But this is not about turning your office into a 1990s Benetton ad for the sake of kindness. Organizations do this all the time. They collect a brown person, an Asian person, someone people might assume to be gay, and maybe even someone with a visible disability, and then they throw these characters together in a photo for the inclusion and diversity (I&D) page on their website, all with cheery smiles to reflect how warm and embracing the organization is.

At its core, everyday inclusion based on earned disclosure is a mandate for high performance. Studies show a direct correlation between employees' views on organizational inclusion efforts and their favorability of the organization as a whole. When they believe the organization actively promotes diversity and inclusion, they are 80 percent more likely to categorize their workplace as high-performing. They are 84 percent more likely to report that their team shares diverse ideas to create innovative solutions.[3]

There is also plenty of evidence to show that diverse and inclusive companies outperform competitors who lag in those qualities. A recent *Wall Street Journal* study found that the five- and ten-year stock returns from companies that scored well on D&I initiatives vastly outpaced those of companies with lower D&I scores.[4] Similarly, a meta-analysis from the American Sociological Association estimates that a mere 1 percent increase in gender and racial diversity results in revenue increases of 3 percent and 9 percent, respectively.[5] That type of demographic diversity, as well as cognitive diversity, is vital—bringing people to the table who see the world from a different point of view and will disagree with you and point out flaws in logic and opportunities you're missing.

But simply bringing diverse perspectives to the table only gets you that Benetton photo for your website. There is powerful research led by Joseph DiStefano, Professor Emeritus of Organizational Behavior and International Business at IMD, that shows diverse teams outperform homogenous teams only when they are well led.[6] If the quality of leadership is equal between those two types of teams, then it is likely that the homogenous team will win the day.

That is because promoting everyday inclusion on diverse teams requires leaders to be qualitatively better than they need to be on homogenous teams. If you increase diversity without increasing the skill of your leadership, problems will emerge—bias, lack of vigilance, careless assumptions, the formation of cliques—all resulting in less-than-optimal individual and collective performance. And you can be assured that those negative results will not be placed at the feet of the inadequate leadership. Instead, people will associate the results with that increase in diversity, fueling suspicion that diversity is the problem.

It is relatively easy to lead homogenous groups. It can be accomplished with basic technical and executive-skill competence because similar people respond to similar solutions. And this is true regardless of the nature of their similarities. However, when you mix introverts with extroverts or creatives with structured thinkers or people from different cultural, linguistic, and regional backgrounds, a cookie-cutter approach will not do. Diverse groups require members to be more thoughtful in their interactions with each other and require leaders specifically to help negotiate relationships within the group. Leaders and colleagues in these groups have to engage in considering aspects of teaming that homogenous teams can get away with ignoring. They must develop strategies to accommodate for differences in communication, tone, approach, motivation, expression, background, experience, and more.

Meeting the challenges of diverse groups can only be done by leaders, not managers. Again, a manager can use technical and executive skills to carry out orders, accomplish tasks, and keep the lights on. But true leaders also deploy emotional labor skills. They work to exude an emotional and psychological state that fortifies and enhances the ability of the diverse people around them to operate effectively, engage with colleagues and organizational goals, and ameliorate internal and external stressors.

There are five interconnected skills involved in a broader definition of *emotional labor* that has expanded beyond the original iteration created by researcher Arlie Hochschild in 1983.

She wrote that emotional labor is the ability to "induce or suppress feeling in order to sustain the outward countenance that produces the proper state of mind in others."[7] If that sounds energy-expensive—you are right. And now, there's more.

Let's start with **emotional literacy**, which is about knowing your feelings, having a sense of empathy for other's feelings, learning to manage our emotions (which is also an element of emotional regulation below) and more, including being able to have a genuine and appropriate, emotional connection with colleagues. In the past, this last element may have been seen "as a bit too much," but in this post-COVID world we've realized that seeing colleagues as real people with emotional lives cannot be discounted.

Then there's **emotional regulation**. This is the process by which people influence the impact of their emotions and the emotional context around them on their actions—from the ability to correctly interpret the emotions we feel and are conveyed in the words and actions of others, to the ability to understand and influence the collective mood and the responses that may be triggered by it. Can you read the room, and can you do something about its tone and the behaviors being triggered? Can you keep the "temperature" where it needs to be?

Next is **metacognition**, and this is complex—and I'll be candid that it's not my expertise area. However, in telling you that I am displaying a metacognitive skill! A key element of metacognition is recognizing the limitations of one's knowledge or ability in a given context—here we mean around this area of the emotional labor of leadership—and then figuring out how to expand that knowledge or extend the ability. People who know their strengths and weaknesses in these areas will be more likely to, as John D. Bransford, Anne L. Brown, and Rodney R. Cocking say in their book *How People Learn*, "actively monitor their learning strategies and resources and assess their readiness for particular tasks and performances."[8] This means that when we know the limits of our abilities—and I do mean their day-to-day fluctuations—we can ensure that we don't bite off more than we can chew. At the least, we can ensure that we understand when our emotional labor resources as leaders may not be equal to the task. Knowing your own mental and emotional state through consistent introspection is essential because that informs the quality of your decision making and communication tone and efficacy.

Another element is **response inhibition**. If your team is truly diverse, you will inevitably find yourself in unfamiliar and even uncomfortable territory. Knee-jerk reactions will not be helpful. Difference will always be more energy expensive than sameness— but it also provides more adaptability, more innovation, more creativity, and better outcomes in the face of disruption.

As a colleague or a leader in a diverse team, you will be tested. Simply the way people do things differently will grate. Probably the hallmark facet of executive control is the ability to not be primed or triggered to act by irrelevant stimulus. The "irrelevant" is important here because response inhibition doesn't mean never responding to anything; it simply means knowing and internalizing that some behaviors never warrant a reflexive response and even behaviors that do warrant a response require a thoughtful one.

Next up is **interpersonal vigilance**, something we have talked about a lot in previous chapters, notably Chapter 4. This is about the reframing of your impact and your "size"—whether a colleague or leader, no matter your role or experience, reconfiguring your perception of self to consider that actions that are inconsequential to you may do disproportionate harm to others. From an outburst to simply ignoring or isolating someone, interpersonal vigilance is having a giant's awareness of the impact you have on the people around you.

If you can participate in or build a diverse team populated by people with these emotional labor skills—people who can empathize and manage interpersonal dynamics—and encourage people to work through friction constructively—that is the difference between success and failure. That team will wildly outperform well-led homogenous teams. But if that same team is instead led by a perfunctory manager, it will fail to outperform even the most homogenous one.

Noninclusive behavior is a poison that stalls innovation, productivity, and collaboration. Its consequences may not be as obvious as poor technical performance or absenteeism, but be assured that you'll get those, too, if inclusion is not addressed. And while it must be applied universally, everyday inclusion is also necessary for recruiting, retaining, and developing employees from protected categories. There are a couple of reasons for this that should be obvious.

The first is an ugly reality that gets no less repugnant by ignoring it. In most cases, "minorities", including people whose identities are considered "protected categories" by law, comprise a tiny fraction of an organization's workforce. And oftentimes, if that fraction is larger, they will occupy service or administrative-level jobs. So the reality is that, if you are employed and reading this book, there is a good chance that your organization has limited experience or expertise with people in these minority categories. This puts those people at an immediate disadvantage. They are in an environment where the majority of their peers share have similar and familiar experiences and backgrounds and have never had to consider or contend with how they are differentially perceived by the world. That majority is often, if not usually, white and straight—but make no bones about it, whatever the nature of the majority, people not in their number are likely to feel othered.

So when minority employees join your ranks, it is natural and predictable that additional effort will be needed to help them feel authentically included. But there's another reason that additional effort is needed to create inclusive environments for minority employees: organizations are terrible at it!

We saw this through the response to the murder of George Floyd in May 2020. Although overwhelmingly warm and well-meaning in their press releases, many organizations had a revelation in just how ill-equipped they were to create an inclusive culture for ethnic minorities in their midst.

It's bewildering, really. And I say this not only from personal experience, though I'd feel confident doing so. Talk to most employees who are different from the majority and they'll have a list at the ready of moments they were slighted, marginalized, and otherwise othered in the workplace. Beyond the anecdotal are studies that indicate just over one-third of minority employees "never or rarely feel close to others." Another 45 percent "think they rarely or never get the support they need to cope with the issues affecting them at work." And 20 percent "never or rarely feel useful" and report "never being able to deal with problems well" in the workplace.[9]

Everyday inclusion is a radical gift that anyone can give. It's a belief that everyone has something unique to contribute. It's looking past packaging and maybe even baggage. There's a scene in *Mary Poppins* where she's moving into her new room in the Banks' house. She opens her carpetbag and starts pulling out a hat rack and a wall mirror, a plant, and even a floor lamp—all useful stuff you'd never expect to find in there. It's actually a decent metaphor for the brain—it's often hard to believe that a near-endless supply of information and insight can be contained in such small things. And this is how we'd like our people to approach work and solve problems, right? Whatever your experience is, whatever you've got in your carpetbag of tricks, whatever you have that might help, dump it out on the table—we want to see it. We *need* to see it to provide one facet of a solution.

Of course, there is risk associated with dumping everything on the table. When Mary pulled out her belongings, any number of things could've spilled out. Her ADHD medication. A Dungeons & Dragons board game. A copy of the Koran. A photo of her wife. Any big or small piece of her most sacred possession, her identity.

When people are encouraged to share their ideas freely, bits of identity are likely to come draped in the essence of who we are. And if they are in an environment where they cannot be confident that those bits won't be scorned or denigrated or mocked, they will hold back. So, instead of emptying their bag to sift through solutions and innovations, they will select their offerings reluctantly and cautiously. It's not that they don't want to contribute. It's just that disclosure is yet unearned, so they proceed with care, lest they pull out something that exposes their otherness. Something that calls into question whether they are a true "fit" with the group.

Groups are obsessed with "fit." *Is this person a good fit with us? Are they the "right" fit? Are they really one of us? Are they a "fit" with the way we do things?* Teams don't give a damn about fit—at least not in the way we hear it discussed regularly. They are focused on values and commitment and technical ability, but not a superficial standard of fit.

Unfortunately, a dysfunctional definition of "fit" is all too common in organizations. The idea of a "good fit" works against inclusion every step of the way, from recruitment to retention to succession planning, and including the scope of clients or customers that an organization will pursue. And filtering for fit—for people who in some superficial way are "like us"—sends dangerously assuring messages to a workforce. To those who feel they're owed an environment where they never have to consider or engage with the presence of difference, it says:

> Fear not, we will not rock your boat. You don't want to spend one iota of energy being more vigilant of your own habitual mindset, language, and behavior, and we're not going to make you.

To the pseudo-traditionalists, it says:

> We have heard your sophisticated defense of the indefensible, and we agree. Preservation of the status quo is the preservation of personal comfort. And even though it is thoroughly at odds with the drive for high performance as an individual or a team, we will never threaten your personal comfort in this way.

To the mediocre but well-integrated middle majority, it says:

> You're good, as always. You're reliably satisfactory, and you understand our policies, procedures, and weaknesses well enough to get the bare minimum done without making waves. That works for us, and our focus on fit will only help to sustain your majority. So good on you, carry on.

And, lastly, to poorly skilled, poorly trained managers, it says:

> Continue to be poorly skilled and poorly trained. We'll make sure you're up to speed on some D&I compliance guidelines, but actual leadership training is a low-yield investment. And why would you need it anyway? We'd never challenge your skills with someone who's not a good fit!

This dysfunctional standard of organizational "fit" has many self-interested benefactors, but it is incompatible with diversity and inclusion and diminishes the talent pool in two serious ways.

First, people who do not fit are dismissed during the interview process, whether for looking or sounding dissimilar to "the norm" for a specific academic or professional background, or for some other perfunctory misalignment. So they're out. Second, there's an entire group of candidates who self-deselect. They are suitable and they are talented, but you'll never know because they're smart enough to read between the lines of the job description—or nowadays they've checked LinkedIn, and the websites rollonfriday.com and glassdoor.com to see what employees *really* think about their companies, and they don't apply.

Explicitly rethinking and redefining "fit" can be a first step toward a culture of everyday inclusion and earned disclosure. A more functional definition—one based on a candidate's alignment with values, ethical standards, shared purpose and strategic objectives—would make space for the most committed and highly skilled people to enhance your organization—even if they were "a bit different." It would embrace the friction of robust idea exchange and the discomfort of organizational evolution. It would push leaders to thrive and win with diversity. It would ensure that "essential" job prerequisites do not unfairly prejudice certain people. It would focus on the results of performance and not the style of performance. That is the kind of "fit" we should strive for.

But, in most workplaces, "good fit" is still interchangeable with "someone like me" or "someone I feel comfortable around." In those environments, people who don't fit will go to great lengths to gain a measure of acceptance or to minimize the attention drawn to themselves and their otherness. They code-switch to blend in or to at least become more invisible. That may seem inconsequential, but in fact you just don't get everything a person has to offer. They censor their appearance, their mindset, their emotions, and their language in ways that are unnatural and unnecessary. And they spend every minute in their job feeling like all of it is packed into a costume that's three sizes too small. It is suffocating, and it's no way to work.

Think about the feeling of relief that comes at the end of a long day when you remove a particularly uncomfortable piece of clothing. That's the relief that everyday inclusion offers: an opportunity to approach work unimpeded by superficial constraints; emotional space that is safe but challenging; the freedom for people to be themselves, reveal themselves, and contribute without inhibition. By welcoming the whole of each individual, inclusive environments encourage proper teaming and nurture innovation.

While I'm cautious of parallels between the real world and my basketball career, I cannot believe it coincidental that the years I spent on the Orlando Magic between 1999 and 2001 were my most productive, both individually and from a team perspective. Our head coach, Glenn "Doc" Rivers, had an appreciation of inclusion and earned disclosure that, for an NBA coach, was ahead of his time. He created a culture that allowed players to be multidimensional, and we all bought in. I was the odd British dude who liked poetry and sci-fi and was always reading and writing during downtime as I worked toward my PhD. A fish out of water. But my eccentricities and my academic ambition were never held against me. In fact, they were embraced. I made it clear that I was a team player and dedicated to our vision. I put in the work on the court and in the weight room and in film sessions. I fulfilled my end of the deal. And, in return, my coaches and teammates permitted me to be myself. We all did that for one other. I may have been the most atypical professional athlete on the team, but it was filled with weirdos and complex characters.

Their respect for who I was off the court enhanced my performance on it. I didn't need to waste energy battling perceptions or trying to "fit." I wasn't paranoid about what was being said about me. I wasn't expecting to be betrayed or stabbed in the back. I could channel everything into basketball, the job at hand. And I could feel confident that, if the team accepted my funny way of speaking and my interests, which to them were unusual, then they might also accept other aspects of who I was.

So, when I eventually came out to those teammates as gay, it was not that big a deal. People misunderstand "coming out of the closet." Very few LGBTQ+ people are in one day and out the next. It is a gradual expansion of trust, a disclosure made again and again. I sold my first book by "coming out" ten years ago, but I was already out to hundreds of people by then. And even though the book made news and was widely read, that was a long time ago. New people enter my life all the time, often unaware of my history. So there are still occasional coming out moments when I present that Fabergé egg and trust that it won't be shattered.

With my Magic teammates, coming out happened 35,000 feet above the ground. We were on a routine team flight, and I was zoned into my schoolwork. Eventually, I looked up from my laptop and noticed that no one was in their usual seats. All of the players were gathered together at the front of the plane, huddled and chatting. I returned to my work and tried to act as though I hadn't even noticed. As though I had no interest in what everyone on the team might be discussing in my absence.

A few minutes later, though, one of our veteran players strolled down the center aisle and stopped at my seat. "Meech," he said, "you don't talk much about women."

I looked up at him and I smiled. "Indeed," I replied.

And he said, "Cool. Just checking." And that was it. Meech was gay. Confirmed.

He returned to my teammates and appeared to relay the news, and there wasn't much reaction one way or another. We all went about our business. It was a weighty and meaningful turning point, and yet it was astoundingly simple. I had, over time, grown more and more comfortable sharing my idiosyncrasies with my teammates. And I could do so because not even once did they make me regret it. So when the time came to share this piece of me that was so fragile and so dear, I gave it up with nary a thought.

What a feeling, that relief and joy as the costume loosens and is eventually shed altogether! There are so many rewards to be gained in a culture of everyday inclusion based upon earned disclosure. But there are so many people who will actively work against it, people who enjoy an embedded entitlement to comfort that is detrimental to progress and innovation. For them, equality and inclusion can feel like oppression. Do not underestimate their power, and do not cower before their influence.

If you can keep this promise and instill a spirit of everyday inclusion into your workplace, you will see the difference. It will not be easy. But you will see the change. Detractors will see it as well and will dismiss your efforts as political correctness. But don't be swayed by their nonsense. In fact, what they're seeing is the beginnings of meritocracy. A threat to their lot but an opportunity and a gift to all.

CHAPTER 14

I Promise to Create an Environment That People Never Want to Leave

When I reflect on that Orlando Magic team, I'm reminded of an intangible quality that is hard to define but a clear hallmark of high-performing teams. Put simply, it was a team that I never wanted to leave.

Management and coaches and teammates and support personnel all worked together to check the traditional boxes for team success. Trust. Transparency. Individual agency. Psychological safety. Clear and consistent communication. But the net effect of that was a uniquely secure and nourishing environment. One that was joyful. One from which I could not be lured away.

I could have left in 2000, and some might say I should have. I was a free agent, and the Los Angeles Lakers offered a contract that guaranteed a few more years and millions more dollars than what Orlando could afford. Accepting the offer would mean upgrading from a fringe playoff team with unproven potential to a legitimate championship contender and the chance to play alongside Shaq and Kobe, future Hall of Famers known by just one name like Larry and Magic.

The Lakers could promise financial security and the chance to compete for a ring. But they could not promise what I knew I would give up if I left Orlando. I was loyal to that organization, but I had also been around long enough to appreciate how rare it was to find an actual team in every meaningful sense of the word. How could I give it up?

In the NBA, one way that you know you're on a team is by the way it responds to success and failure. This is true in other workplaces as well, but the response is particularly transparent on a basketball court under the gaze of 20,000 fans. On a true team, when a shot is made—whether it's a simple lay-up resulting from a well-orchestrated play or an improvised and acrobatic shot with a higher degree of difficulty—you will see the person who made it point to the teammate who passed the ball. And that teammate, in turn, will likely point to the teammate who freed him up to make the pass. And by the time the team has returned to the defensive end of the court, all five players will have received a point or a fist bump or a pat on the rear. The player credited with the two points takes the adulation of the crowd—the respect and praise of those watching—and makes sure it's distributed to the entire team. The success is publicly shared, and it's clear to anyone watching that the made basket was a team effort, even when it wasn't. Even when the shot was in truth a demonstration of individual greatness.

This is not the response you see from groups of elite athletes who happen to wear the same uniform. In those situations, when someone makes a shot, they will turn to the crowd and soak up the applause like a solar panel absorbing sunlight. There is no acknowledgment of anyone else's contribution to the achievement. Finger-pointing happens only after a missed shot or a missed defensive assignment. Publicly shared failure. Sometimes it's a subtle eye roll. Sometimes it is a more direct grimace or scowl or an exacerbated waving of the arms. *Why did you set the screen on that side? Why did you pass the ball toward my knees rather than my chest? Why didn't you rotate quicker on defense?* The message sent to all of those fans is: *I may have botched that, but you should be aware that someone else screwed up, too.*

On a team, when that shot or defensive rotation is missed or an errant pass is thrown, there is shared public accountability. The most obvious culprit might pat his own chest and signal *my bad, my bad.* But then you'll see a teammate shake him off and say *no, no, my bad, my bad. I got you.* And that teammate may have contributed to the error or not. But, on a team, it doesn't matter, at least in public. Because teams know something that groups don't know, and that is, in the grand scheme of things, if you leave one person to shoulder all the blame, they are less able to function. The weight of an error can be too heavy for one person to bear in public. It will crush an individual. When the entire group carries that weight, you know they are a team.

That was the type of support that I enjoyed with those Magic teams. And I say "enjoy" quite deliberately. No matter how talented a group of individuals is, a well-led optimized team will kick its ass. And they will have fun doing it! Nothing can replace the sheer joy of being part of a team, as opposed to a group of elite individuals. When you're in difficult times together, it is remarkable. And when you win together, it is transcendent.

This final promise is to create an environment that people never want to leave—because they've found a place where they are seen and heard and valued. A place where they'll receive constructive feedback but won't be abandoned should they fail, where they are never alone and never expected to be a specific, superficial "fit" in order to belong. Put together all of the ingredients that we've discussed—inclusion, trust, psychological safety, attentiveness—and sprinkle in a healthy dose of joyfulness, and the result will be a potent mix that, when consumed, can be highly addictive. People will respond because they will recognize how precious and rare it is.

I remember my first taste, and it was almost accidental, prompted by a chance encounter with a complete stranger. As a teenager, I would take the bus from our flat in Stockport to the library in Manchester. And after I stocked up on books, I would stop at Gregg's, a lunch chain in the UK that sells what they call Steak Bakes, which are pastry puffs filled with gravy and beef. They're quite delicious, though not much for nutritional benefit and not really intended for high-volume consumption. But at 17, my hands were so large that I could wedge one between each finger. So I would do just that and board the bus home with my books in one hand and three or four Steak Bakes in the other.

One day, I was walking to the bus with both hands full. By then, I had learned to walk briskly and limit my focus to avoid the peripheral laughter and the expressions of horror and fear—pixelating the world in order to get from point A to point B without being reminded that I was a freak. On this particular day, though, an older man stepped directly in my path and stopped me short. I was sure that he was going to ask how the weather was up there or make some other terrible joke. People made all kinds of ridiculous comments to me. But instead this man said, "You know, you would be *great* at basketball."

I remember his phrasing precisely because it was so effective. He didn't say, "You should play basketball." When someone says you should do or should be something, it often sounds like they're insinuating that the "something" is actually the only thing you're good for. Even at 50 years old, I'm still told by strangers that I should play basketball, a suggestion that is ironic on top of insulting and depressing. This man didn't say that, though. Nor did he say, "Would you like to play basketball?" If he had, I would've replied, "Sir, I have five unread books and two remaining Steak Bakes that I'd like to return to. You can keep your basketball, thank you."

Instead, he said, "You would be *great* at basketball." And it was puzzling yet tantalizing. Outside of my mother and sisters, people had rarely suggested that I could be worth much of anything. Yet here was a suggestion that I could be *great*. Here was a person who reflected back to me not a monster but, rather, someone with potential. *Great*, you say? Tell me more.

He explained a bit about basketball. Like most people in England, I hadn't heard of it before. But he laid out the basics and gave me some information about a local gym where children my age gathered to play.

I showed up at that gym about a week later, wearing the rugby kit that all male students were issued at our school and a pair of plimsolls, which were simple canvas low-top shoes. It was raining, and I stood outside for a while staring through the glass door.

I could hear the squeaking of shoes and the bouncing of the ball and the chatter and laughter of school-aged children—all stuff that I traditionally withdrew from. And I remember pushing that door open and imagining the rabbit hole from *Alice's Adventures in Wonderland* as I stepped through. Where was I going? What was I doing?

I walked into the actual gymnasium, and as soon as I was spotted the action stopped. All of the children turned to me and froze in place for just a second or two, letting the ball bounce bounce bounce and roll away. I had a notion to turn and flee because they were all staring at me and it seemed it would only be a moment before they pulled out the torches and pitchforks. But then one yelled, "You're on *our* team!" And they all started running toward me, screaming over each other, "No, he's on our team!" "We get him!" "We want him!"

They were grabbing at me, trying to literally drag me into their ranks. And it was such an unusual feeling to be coveted in this way. My heart nearly exploded. But I also felt guilty because I had never touched a basketball and thus had little to offer as a team-mate. People assume that height automatically translates to talent on a basketball court, but there are plenty of towering stiffs who can barely compete in a YMCA pickup game. Being tall is useful, but not without tens of thousands of hours spent practicing and developing skills. And, once we settled on which team I'd join, I began proving this point.

My first play was a thud and a clap. They passed me the ball and it hit me in the chest. I whiffed completely, clapping my hands together too late. Thud. Clap. The next time it came my way, I caught the ball but had no idea what to do with it. So I just stood there feeling somewhat triumphant for not having missed it again, holding it above my head where no one could reach. *Shoot it! Shoot it!* My teammates were pointing toward the hoop and eventually realized their instructions were falling on deaf ears. I didn't know what it meant to shoot it. *Throw the ball up there, into the net!*

195

What happened next was magical. I pivoted toward the hoop and let it fly. It was one of those moments when time stands still. The ball suspended in the air, rotating and rotating before sailing by the rim and then the backboard, missing its target altogether and flying out of bounds. But the magical part came when one of the boys retrieved the ball and, smiling, said to the group, "My God! His first shot and he only missed by six feet!"

Nowadays, thanks to the work of Carol Dweck, we might say that reaction was reflective of a "growth mindset." Recognition of a potential that, through discipline and hard work, could develop into something more. But, back then, it just felt like kindness. Even when I screwed up, these people wanted me to keep trying. To be more involved. They didn't seem to mind my failures. Every time I looked into their eyes, I saw my potential reflected back. For once, I did not see fear or ridicule. I did not see the Hunchback. I saw people who wanted to see me succeed. I saw people who, if anything, wished they could be like me. What an unfamiliar but glorious sight!

More than anything, that feeling of acceptance and support was what led me to basketball. I would later learn of the educational opportunities the sport could provide and the fortunes it could lead to. But that initial sense of belonging lit the spark.

When we finished playing, we took off our shoes and sat on the gym floor laughing and learning about each other. And some of the boys started telling me about the NBA, where the best basketball players in the world compete. My imagination ran wild. I was already convinced that I never wanted to lose the feeling I had sitting there. But, if that's how it felt playing pickup in a dingy, stinky gym, then what must the NBA feel like? I had to find out. So less than an hour after my first shot, I told my new friends I was going to play in the NBA. And none of them questioned it. None of them thought I was crazy. *Yes*, they said, *you should! Let's do it!* I was blown away by their enthusiasm. *Let's*, they said! They wanted to participate in my journey. They wanted to contribute to my success!

I never wanted that feeling to end; I never wanted to leave. I would have sat on the floor in my socks forever. By nature, I liked books and pie and reclined positions held for extended periods of time. But this new world required vegetables and sweat and weight lifting—all of which I'd actively avoided. That would have to change, though, because I had to hang on to that feeling.

Such is the power of inclusion. It can inspire a fat kid from Stockport to be among the world's best at a sport he's not even interested in, and, in fact, is mostly bored by. That's an amazing piece of this. The end goal almost doesn't matter. It can be contrary to a person's interests and personality. When we are surrounded by people who make us feel valuable and bolster our spirit, we will perform even the most tedious work to high standards. It is quite common for people to find their careers by happenstance. They end up in a field that perhaps they didn't even know existed when they were younger and dreaming of what they'd one day be. When you are fortunate enough to find an environment where you are authentically connected to people who nurture and challenge you—where you enjoy autonomy yet are never left to feel alone— no work is too boring or monotonous, whether it's stocking shelves or entering data or throwing a ball into a hole. The destination is incidental. You just want to travel with that group for a journey that never ends.

These environments are sacred and highly addictive. And, for that reason, they can be a bit dangerous. With mixed results, I spent my basketball career trying to recapture the pure feeling of joy and inclusion that I felt when I was just learning the game. It was not unlike a junkie who is in constant pursuit of a high that matches the one that first got him hooked. Fortunately, I had the support of family and coaches who kept me in line. Because, had they not, I might have taken drastic measures to acquire or retain that feeling. I might have skipped class to spend more time at the gym. I might have used performance-enhancing drugs. I might have declined an opportunity with a different team even though it was more lucrative and personally beneficial. Wait, I did do that one!

Promise to create an environment that people never want to leave. It's an ambitious responsibility but utterly doable. People want to be led. They want to be held in giant hands. They want the heat shield and safe harbor that a giant's shadow affords. And each of us can offer that in some way.

There is something transcendent about being around people who recognize the breadth and depth of your value. People who do the work of building familiarity. People who drive us but genuinely care about our welfare. We never want to leave those people. And we will work better and harder for and among them than we will for people who view us as machines of convenience. It's a natural human inclination and always will be.

In 1940, Charlie Chaplin released *The Great Dictator*, a political satire in which Chaplin plays two protagonists who bear a striking resemblance: an impoverished Jewish barber and a Hitleresque dictator. The film is Chaplin's first "talkie," and he used it to deliver an impassioned message that remains profound yet so simple. It comes at the end of the film when, through a comedy of circumstances, the barber is mistaken for the dictator and is forced to address a massive crowd. He stands on the stage, nervous at first. But, summoning courage, he dives into the role and announces a change of heart, denouncing tyranny on the tyrant's behalf.

"I don't want to rule or conquer people," he says.

"I should like to help everyone if possible. We all want to help one another. Human beings are like that. We want to live by each other's happiness—not by each other's misery. We don't want to hate and despise one another. In this world, there is room for everyone. And the good earth is rich and can provide for everyone. The way of life can be free and beautiful, but we have lost the way."[1]

This is the human compulsion, to help. There is room for everyone. But we have lost the way.

"Greed has poisoned men's souls, has barricaded the world with hate, has goose-stepped us into misery and bloodshed. We have developed speed, but we have shut ourselves in.

Machinery that gives us abundance has left us in want. Our knowledge has made us cynical. Our cleverness, hard and unkind. We think too much and feel too little. More than machinery, we need humanity. More than cleverness, we need kindness and gentleness."[2]

That deep and authentic appreciation for humanity is essential. It was essential in 1940, and it will be in 2040. You can't create the environments we're talking about without it. And remember, we're not creating these environments just to make people feel good. We're creating them because they're proven to be the most conducive to achieving successful results. That reality won't change either.

Much will change. Much is changing. In years to come, there will be significantly less need for massive towers, centralized in major city centers, filled with thousands of employees from one company. We will see more contingent and project workers. More transient workers, more people working from home, and more digital nomads whose location changes with their mood as much as their client or project. Within industries and job categories, the qualifications and portfolios of candidates are going to shift and, according to McKinsey, up to 375 million people globally are going to need to move out of their current occupational category or role to find sustainable work.[3] And yes, the nature and composition of pay and benefits and organizational design are going to shift radically, too.

So when people are deciding where they'd like to spend their working hours, the decision will rely heavily on where they feel the best. How does this particular manager and this constellation of colleagues make me feel when I work for this company?

Again, this is not a question of "snow-flakery"; it's about the fact that we will *all* still be working incredibly hard, but the place that offers you an authentic, collegial, and team-based experience while you are facing those challenges *together* is going to win out.

Perhaps you're wondering whether the interpersonal and team experience matters if all of our interactions will happen through a computer screen?

Yes, it will.

The importance and relevance of the human experience in work will be universal, even in industries where you might think otherwise. In hospitals, for example, doctors will be able to perform certain work using remote technology. With an Internet connection and virtual reality goggles, they will be able to engage with robots, clinicians, and patients without having to be based in any one hospital. So where they choose to work will be determined less by geography and more by who they'll be working with—not just which surgical group is the most lucrative or pleasant to spend their working hours with, but which creates the least additional cognitive burden, which adds the most additional value to their experience and on and on.

As we are increasingly physically distanced from those we work with, interpersonal skills are ironically becoming even more valuable. The importance of authentic and humane leadership is on the rise, and yet the ease of demonstrating it is falling through the floor. When you've got everyone in that one big office tower, it's not particularly difficult to ensure that everyone feels connected at least once in a while. You can wait until your paths inevitably cross in a hallway or elevator to attempt some niceties or you can try catered lunches, a surprise cake in the afternoon, some after-hours drinks. But when people are scattered across countries and time zones, it takes greater effort and intentionality to create and preserve those connections.

While much is still unknown about the years and decades to come, the future of work will most certainly be *human*. Technology and innovation and artificial intelligence will continue to advance and astound—and both will remain in need of constant human scrutiny. Roles will change and some—perhaps entire sectors— will become redundant, as has happened a hundred times before in our history. But the future of work is and will continue to be human.

Epilogue

Hoover the Landing

I hope that you're eager to start fulfilling these promises, and that you're convinced the work they demand is both within your ability and absolutely critical. Commit to that work fully. Commit to consistency in behavior and congruence between words and deeds, day in and day out. There are no breaks for giants.

As we part, I'd like to invoke the memory of my mother one last time. I hold her up as an example so frequently because, more than anyone I've ever known, she understood the labor and responsibility associated with authentic, transformational leadership. She appreciated the extraordinary impact that could be made by otherwise ordinary people. And through each stage of her life, Mum demonstrated leadership that was purposeful and unmistakable yet humble and selfless.

She was not one to insist upon herself. Before having children, she traveled with my father to his birth country of Nigeria to support the rebel Igbo fighters in the Biafran War. In the face of grave danger, she courageously provided frontline medical aid until the government forces overwhelmed and starved out the resistance. She and my father were driven out of Nigeria on foot, dodging gunfire and eating grubs to survive. But she never spoke about this extraordinary episode. That was not her style. If she were alive today, she would not be writing LinkedIn essays about the lemon water she drinks at 5am as Step 2B of her proven morning routine. Her only interest was walking the walk.

She aspired to be a leader not because of the power or status it ascribed but because of the impact that she could make on others. She viewed her legacy as the achievements of those she influenced and was uninterested in her personal accomplishments. After living with cancer for several years, she became terminally ill during my senior season at Penn State. She would become indignant with reporters who asked her whether it added to her suffering to be separated by her son playing ball overseas. She would have it no other way, she'd tell them. The entire job of a mother is to help her children realize their goals and achieve the lives they want and need. She knew that me playing in the USA was part of that, and she was adamant that it not be interrupted, even and especially by her illness.

Mum was remarkably consistent. In good times and bad, when stakes were high and when no one was watching, her perspective on life and her respect for others held steady. And she demanded that consistency from her children as well. Our father left the family when my sisters and I were quite young. On most days, Mum would leave for work before we woke and would return home after we were already in bed. She was a low-ranking general practitioner, and we would sometimes go for days without seeing her. To keep the house and family in order, she assigned tasks to my older sisters and me, clearly scheduled on a whiteboard hung on the wall and updated from week to week—dish washing, meal preparation, taking out the rubbish, and so on.

Sometimes I would miss her desperately. On one occasion when I was about 13, I decided I had to stay up past bedtime just so I could greet her and give her a hug. It's all I wanted to do. My sisters went about their business that evening, eating dinner, completing their tasks, and eventually heading to bed. But all I could think about was how much I missed Mum and how badly I wanted to tell her that I loved her and appreciated the hard she work she did for us. So, after we ate, I took a seat at the foot of the stairs leading up to our bedrooms, and I waited there as night fell and the room grew dark. I sat there for hours.

Eventually, I heard the jingling and jangling outside our flat, which always signaled her arrival. She carried a huge key ring that she said she'd use as a weapon if someone ever tried to mug her, a possibility that to me seemed unlikely. Even though I'd already passed her in height, I saw my mother as enormous and formidable. No one would mess with her.

When I heard those keys, I raced to the door, beaming with love. I adored and missed her, and I needed to tell her so immediately. She walked into the flat, and before she could even drop her bag, I threw my arms around her. A massive bear hug. And she hugged me back, but I was familiar enough with her hugs to know that something was off. She was holding back. So I hugged her harder, but the harder I hugged, the less she hugged back. And I could tell that she was straining her neck to look past my shoulder, as if something had caught her eye.

I released our embrace, and she kept looking beyond me, placing her bag and keys on the table. "I'm sorry, Mum," I said, eagerly. "I know I should be in bed, but I haven't seen you in three days and I needed to hug you and tell you how much I love you."

Had she even heard me? She glanced at me for a moment, but then right back over my shoulder to the wall, where our schedule was hanging. And she squinted her eyes, short-sighted like me, and matched my name to the day of the week on the matrix and said, "Did you Hoover the landing?"

I had not, I confessed, even though it was my task for the day. "But this is what happened!" I explained. "I came home and all I could think about was how much I love you and miss you when you're out all day. And I couldn't do anything because I was so distracted by how much I've been missing you. I love you so much and just wanted to see you!"

I went in for another hug, but she put her hand on my chest and gently stopped me.

"Son," she said, "if you love me, you'd Hoover the landing."

Those words sound a bit cold—cruel, even—written on the page and detached from her voice. But I understood straightaway the point she was making. Here she was, working to exhaustion day after day so that my sisters and I could want for nothing. And, in return, she asked for little more than completion of some very basic tasks. So I could carry on rhapsodically about how much I loved her. But, on that day, I chose to blow off the one commitment that I'd made to her and our family. I didn't Hoover the landing.

What Mum wanted and valued most highly was congruence between words and behavior. It's what most of us want. And when we don't see that congruence consistently, we put up walls. You can tell people they're valued and they're the bedrock of your organization, but, if your actions consistently fail to support that sentiment, they will notice. If you even occasionally treat people as an afterthought, they will be disinclined to connect on your terms when you need them. They'll be less willing to give extra. They will do just enough.

Rhetoric unsupported by consistent behavior will not cut it. You've got to Hoover the landing, every day. Inconsistent leadership breeds mistrust and skepticism. It has the effect that infidelity does on a relationship. When you're in love, your partner might come into the bedroom before you've woken up and put a rose on your pillow. And you'll be intoxicated by its scent as you awake, and maybe they've also put a hot cup of tea by the bed. And perhaps they kiss you on the cheek. And the combination of these simple expressions has the power to ignite a rush of chemicals and hormones that leave you euphoric.

But when your partner cheats, that euphoria is harder to access. Even if you're able to reconcile to some degree, it will take quite some time for those same expressions to bear a similar effect. The chemicals and hormones are short-circuited by the knowledge of what your partner has done to hurt you. Maybe it was six months ago, and maybe it was ten years ago, but you know that what they did once they could do again. You know what they're capable of.

Making good on our promises requires disciplined and unconditional consistency. People need to be confident that their colleagues and superiors are all on a level playing field, held to clear and equal standards—standards that are respectful to others and inclusive and empathetic, standards that, when violated, are defended by meaningful sanctions that are well understood in advance. If a person misbehaves and nothing happens, it sends a message to everyone. If a person is mistreated and nothing happens, it sends a message. It signals that organizational standards only apply to certain people. Values are upheld only when it's convenient.

The American comedian Jon Stewart said, "If you don't stick to your values when they're being tested, they're not values. They're hobbies." The application of these promises cannot be a hobby. It can't get your focus only on days when you have the energy or a little more space in your diary.

In my playing days, I would occasionally cut corners during our weight room sessions. Even the most elite athletes do this occasionally. You get immersed in your workout and you're pushing your body to the brink. And then between reps you notice that the attention of your teammates and coaches and trainers is all focused elsewhere. And so you dial it down for a moment, just a smidge. It's such an incremental adjustment that most people could barely detect it. Maybe you go from 100 percent exertion to 95 percent—just enough to catch a breath, but not so much that you can't quickly ratchet it back to 100 should anyone turn their eye to you.

I remember giving myself one of those quick reprieves during a session and thinking myself quite clever. But I had a trainer named Warren, who was quiet and astute. And at the end of our workout, Warren tapped me on the shoulder and whispered one concise phrase that I've never forgotten: "You're always being observed."

You're always being observed. It's really that simple. In professional sports, that constant observation and scrutiny is more obvious. There are statistics and advanced metrics to measure your contributions to the team. And coaches maintain depth charts for each position, which make clear where everyone stands in relation to their teammates. A couple weeks into my first preseason in Orlando, I was alarmed to see my name at the bottom of the lists for both positions I played. Overall, there were 18 of us competing for 15 spots, so I had some work to do. I was being observed, and the coaches didn't like what they were seeing.

So I decided to start practicing out of their sight. I would attend our regular practices at the team facility, but then I'd walk to a public gym where I could put in additional work, doing drills and shooting and conditioning, all without further exposing my deficiencies to the coaching staff. I did that supplemental workout in the public gym every day. And one day I was taking a water break on the sidelines when I noticed two kids shooting at the next court. It struck me as odd because it was a weekday at a time when they should have been in school. But in between shots, they kept looking toward me with that passive wanting expression that every leader should recognize. It's that look that people give when they're afraid to approach you but are also hoping beyond hope that you'll reach out to them. So I did.

I didn't want to, honestly. I was hyper-focused on the depth chart, and every minute that wasn't spent climbing from the bottom of it seemed like wasted time. But I had a fleeting thought of my mother and what she would expect me to do in the situation. In accordance with that, even though it irritated me to interrupt my work, I called the boys over with a wave.

Just that one act of waving lit them up. They sprinted across the court to me, as if running on air. They had no idea who I was, but I had *seen* them and I had not turned away. I had acknowledged them, and, with huge smiles, they introduced themselves, Chris and Eric. They looked to be about 10 or 11, and they were brothers. "Nice to meet you," I said. "Shouldn't you be in school?" They said no, but they didn't offer any further explanation. And then they begged to play against me, two against one, which I obliged.

A kinder giant might have shown some mercy to young Chris and Eric, but I destroyed them. Block, dunk, repeat. Devastation rained down from all angles, as it will when a fully grown six foot ten man is challenged by 10- and 11-year-old boys. Really, though, decisive victory was the quickest way to get back to training so I made short work of them. And when it was done, they thanked me and scurried off and I returned to my shooting drills.

A couple days later, I saw them again and a similar scene played out. This time, I invited them right over when I was ready for a break. "Chris! Eric!" I called with a wave. "Let's go!"

Again they sprinted over, again I asked about school, and again they pushed that question aside. Again, we played two on one, and again, I murdered them. And so it went, for the next couple of weeks. But, over time, they started revealing more about themselves and why they weren't in school. By then I'd spent hundreds of hours working with "at-risk" kids at Penn State. But I would learn that Chris and Eric came from a family situation that was as challenging and tragic as any I'd encountered in State College. Their parents were alive, but the boys were essentially alone in the world, fending for themselves without a family.

Also over time, I started ascending up the depth chart. When the final cuts were made, I survived, and by the end of the season I had broken into the starting lineup. But what remained of my family was thousands of miles away. And with few friends in Orlando, I had no one to take my complimentary game tickets, which are allotted to each player. So usually I'd leave them for Chris and Eric. They spent my first season in Orlando in the family section and family lounge, cheering, eating, and laughing alongside the parents and spouses and children of my teammates.

We were three orphans, for all intents and purposes. But I looked out for them and spent time with them and convinced them to take school seriously. We effectively became family to each other, to the point that, in the summertime, I brought them home to England to attend my basketball camp—an invitation that unwittingly made the family status official.

I was coaching a group of campers when I heard a scream from the adjacent court, followed by a burst of commotion. It was Chris, and he was writhing on the floor with what turned out to be a broken ankle. Soon enough, we were loading him into an ambulance and he was screaming because he was so scared but intermittently laughing from the nitrous oxide. It was an odd combination, and as we rode to the hospital, I was already wondering what I'd gotten myself into. We arrived, and they admitted him and rolled him off to surgery to set the bone. But just before they did, he grabbed my arm and pulled down the little oxygen mask covering his face.

"Will you take care of us?" he asked. What a question. It put me on the spot and even felt a little manipulative in the moment. But what are preteens if not manipulative? I knew what he meant by "take care of us." I knew that he and his brother yearned for something permanent, something reliable. I knew they wanted someone who could be a father. And though I took a sleepless night to think about it, I eventually said yes. We returned to the States, and after about six weeks of paperwork and legalities, I adopted Chris and Eric as my own.

Fast-forward and they are now in their 30s with five children between them. A few years ago, we spent Thanksgiving together at Chris's home. After dinner, they took me out to the balcony to smoke a cigar and chat, which is what happens in America after Thanksgiving dinner. Everyone eats, and then the men stand around outside and drink and smoke and chat. That's my understanding, at least.

But during that chat, there was a pause, a moment of silence. And then one of them asked, "Do you know why it was that we chose you?" The question seemed odd because I was pretty sure I had chosen them. But I played along and answered with the most obvious response. "Because I was in the NBA? Because I was making a shit ton of money?"

"No," Chris said, both of them laughing. "You weren't even that good."

So was it the seriousness with which I approached their guardianship? I asked. My responsible and nurturing care? The fact that I had gotten them back to school and created opportunities that saved them from a less desirable fate?

No, they said again, followed by more laughter. It wasn't any of that.

"Do you remember that first time we met?" Chris asked. "And you asked us our names?"

"Yes, of course," I said.

"And do you remember the *second* time we met? It was a couple days later, and you still remembered our names?"

"Yes," I replied. "I remember."

"Well, that was it. We knew you were going to be the one because you remembered our names. That was why we chose you."

I was floored by that insight. I'd ended up with this joyful extension of my family simply because I spared some time when I thought other things were a priority, and I remembered two names.

I share this anecdote in closing as one last reminder of the profound impact that giants can have through seemingly inconsequential actions. By keeping these promises, you can positively shape the way that people view themselves. You can make people feel connected. You can unleash their talent.

And while you are not the intended beneficiary, honoring these promises will lead to rewards that you could never imagine. They can make an NBA starter, a globe-trotting organizational psychologist, and a grandfather of five out of a fat, shy, queer, half-geek, half-nerd boy, buried in books and pie.

The world is filled with unique, bizarre, and wonderful people with diverse gifts and reservoirs of untapped potential. Promise to be an ally to them and an advocate for them. Promise to be a true colleague and an authentic leader and to bring out the best in them. Promise a healthy but competitive passion for winning.

And keep these promises, unconditionally and persistently. That is the duty and the honor of being a giant.

Notes

Chapter 3

1 Harkin, B., Webb, T., & Chang, B. (2016) Does monitoring goal progress promote goal attainment? A meta-analysis of the experimental evidence, *American Psychological Association* 142(2): 198–229.

Chapter 4

1 Bertrand, M., & Mullainathan, S. (2004) Are Emily and Greg more employable than Lakisha and Jamal? A field experiment on labor market discrimination, *American Economic Review* 94 (Sept. 4): 991–1013.
2 http://csi.nuff.ox.ac.uk/wp-content/uploads/2019/01/Are-employers-in-Britain-discriminating-against-ethnic-minorities_final.pdf
3 www-2.rotman.utoronto.ca/facbios/file/Whitening%20MS%20R2%20Accepted.pdf.
4 Rosiek, J. (2003) Emotional scaffolding: An exploration of the teacher knowledge at the intersection of student emotion and the subject matter, *Journal of Teacher Education* 54(5): 399–412.

Chapter 8

1 Manyika, J., Lund, S., Chui, M., Bughin, J., Woetzel, J., Batra, P., Ko, R. & Sanghvi, S. (2017) *Jobs lost, jobs gained: What the future of work will mean for jobs, skills, and wages.* [online] McKinsey. Available at: <https://www.mckinsey.com/featured-insights/future-of-work/jobslost-jobs-gained-what-the-future-of-work-will-mean-for-jobs-skillsand-wages>.

Chapter 10

1 Kraus, M., & Huang, C., & Keltner, D. (2010) Tactile communication, cooperation, and performance: An ethological study of the NBA. *Emotion* (Washington, D.C.) 10: 745–9. doi: 10.1037/a0019382.
2 Hackman, J.R. (2002) Why teams don't work. In: Tindale R.S. et al. (eds) *Theory and Research on Small Groups. Social Psychological Applications to Social Issues*, vol 4. Boston, MA: Springer. doi: 10.1007/0-306-47144-2_12.
3 Huckman, R., & Staats, B. (2013) The hidden benefits of keeping teams intact. *Harvard Business Review*. 91: 27–9.

Chapter 11

1 Garthwaite, C., Keener, J., Notowidigdo, M.J., & Ozminkowski, N.F. (2020) Who profits from amateurism? Rent-sharing in modern college sports. National Bureau of Economic Research. Cambridge, MA. Available at: www2.nber.org/papers/w27734.pdf?stream=business&utm_source=newsletter&utm_medium=email&utm_campaign=newsletter_axiosmarkets.

Chapter 12

1 "Avocation." *Merriam-Webster.com Dictionary*, Merriam-Webster, www.merriam-webster.com/dictionary/avocation.
2 *FIFA Disciplinary Code 2019 Edition*, 13.1 https://resources.fifa.com/image/upload/fifa-disciplinary-code-2019-edition.pdf?cloudid=i8zsik8xws0pyl8uay9i.
3 Kotter, J. & Schlesinger, L. (2008) Choosing strategies for change. [online] *Harvard Business Review*. Available at: https://hbr.org/2008/07/choosing-strategies-for-change.

Chapter 13

1 Kahn, W.A. (1990) Psychological conditions of personal engagement and disengagement at work. *Acad. Manag. J.*33: 692–724
2 Edmondson, A.C. (1996) Learning from mistakes is easier said than done: Group and organizational influences on the detection and correction of human error.' *Journal of Applied Behavioral Science*, 32: 5–32.

3 Deloitte (2013) Waiter, is that inclusion in my soup? A new recipe to improve business performance. [online] Available at: https://www2.deloitte.com/content/dam/Deloitte/au/Documents/human-capital/deloitte-au-hc-diversity-inclusion-soup-0513.pdf.

4 Holger, D. (2019) The business case for more diversity, *The Wall Street Journal* (Oct. 26). *Available at*: www.wsj.com/articles/the-business-case-for-more-diversity-11572091200.

5 Herring, C. (2017) Is diversity still a good thing? *American Sociological Review*, 2017;82(4):868–877. doi:10.1177/0003122417716611

6 DiStefano, J.J. & Maznevski, M.L. (2000) Creating value with diverse teams in global management, *Organizational Dynamics* 29(1): 0–63.

7 Hochschild, A. R. (1979) Emotion work, feeling rules, and social structure,' *American Journal of Sociology* 85.(3): 551–575.

8 Bransford, J.D., Brown, A.L., & Cocking, R.R., eds. (1999) *How People Learn: Brain, Mind, Experience, and School.* Washington, DC: National Academy Press.

9 Kandola, P. (2019) Responses to Exclusion. Unpublished paper presented at the BPS Occupational Psychology Conference.

Chapter 14

1 *The Great Dictator*, dir. Charlie Chaplin (United Artists, 1940).

2 Ibid.

3 Manyika, J., Lund, S., Chui, M., Bughin, J., Woetzel, J., Batra, P., Ko, R., & Sanghvi, S. (2017) Jobs lost, jobs gained: What the future of work will mean for jobs, skills, and wages. [online] McKinsey. Available at: https://www.mckinsey.com/featured-insights/future-of-work/jobs-lost-jobs-gained-what-the-future-of-work-will-mean-for-jobs-skills-and-wages.

Acknowledgments

None of these words or stories would be possible without some very special people.

To Muriel and Andy, you took care of me when things were at their bleakest. Without word or question, you enabled my revivification when I thought all was lost. You both inspire me, with lives fraught with challenge you appear to face into them and win.

To Uki, our paths could not be more different, and we live so far apart, but you are and always have been a force of nature and testament to tenacity. I only hope you know that distance has not made my love for you wane.

To Peter, the best I can say is to quote Star Trek (which is almost blasphemy for a Star Wars nerd): "I have been and always will be, your friend" and have felt that reciprocated through the best and worst of times over the last 40 years.

To Julie, you have been through so much yourself and come out on top. Your partnership with me at the rebirth of APS spoke of such ambition all those years ago in Manchester. That we are still partners to this day is a testament to your essential friendship, the value you bring to the business and your eternal patience with me.

To Chris, you are relatively new to my inner circle, but your friendship has been a cause of much joy and camaraderie in my life. Thank you for all those days we walk and sit in silence and watch bad TV – those days refill an empty cup.

To Chris and Eric, your lives are transformed by your individual and collective force of will. To see your success now is an inspiration and while we are separated by an ocean, I hope that a couple of our stories still live in your heads to be shared with your children.

The truth is that someone like me, a geek and a nerd who teaches by telling elaborate stories is no one without people who are willing to listen. In the same way, an author is nothing without people who are willing to read their words. I have been so fortunate to hear back from so many people who have heard at least some of the content of this book in presentations and speeches or in my weekly 'Jedi Reflection' videos and I want to thank you for helping me hone my message. Thank you for telling me how my words and ideas changed your perspectives and thank you for sharing back so many stories of your own that have left me equally transformed.

About the Author

John Amaechi OBE is a respected organisational psychologist, best-selling New York Times author, sought after public speaker, executive coach and the Founder of APS Intelligence Ltd ("APS"). He is a non-executive director of a FTSE 250 food company and a £2.4bn healthcare organisation in addition to being a board advisor for several FTSE100 organisations in the financial, legal and professional services, technology, publishing, engineering and retail sectors. John has been recognised as one of HR's most influential thinkers by HR Magazine.

John grew up in Stockport, near Manchester in the North of England and left for America alone, at the age of 18, to pursue his ambition to become the first Britain to have a career in the NBA. Just six years after picking up a basketball, he achieved that goal and in 2000, he became the only Britain to have his jersey hung in the US Basketball Hall of Fame in Springfield, Massachusetts.

Since retirement from sport, John has continued to learn and teach. He is a Chartered Scientist, a Chartered Fellow of the CIPD and a Fellow of the Royal Society for Public Health and the Association of Business Psychologists. He is a Research Fellow at the University of East London and his research interests include effective, inclusive leadership, building high-performing teams and organisational design that maximises productivity and human thriving in readiness for the future world of work.

John leads a team of psychologists, behavioural scientists and experienced business strategists that design and deliver evidence-based advisory interventions to service clients with people challenges that impact organisational performance.

APS has worked with hundreds of organisations over the last decade developing strategy and enhancing leaders, their teams and organisational culture in companies ranging from rapid scale-ups to established global brands.

Organisations approach APS to understand and unpick complex people challenges through advisory services driven by complex analytics, motivational presentations, workshops and master-classes, executive coaching and digital learning. All of which can be delivered virtually or face-to-face.

Index